Straight &
Crooked
Thinking

Straight & Crooked Thinking

R. H. Thouless & C. R. Thouless

JOHN MURRAY LEARNING

Hodder Education
First published in UK 1930.

This edition published 2011 by Hodder Education, part of Hachette UK, 338 Euston
Road, London NW1 3BH.
14

First edition © 1930 R. H. Thouless
Second edition © 1953 R. H. Thouless
Third edition © 1974 R. H. Thouless
Fourth edition © 1990 R. H. Thouless and C. R. Thouless
Fifth edition © 2011 C. R. Thouless
Reprinted in 2021 by John Murray Learning, an imprint of John Murray Press, a
division of Hodder & Stoughton, an Hachette UK company.

British Library Cataloguing in Publication Data: a catalogue record for this title is
available from the British Library.

Typeset by MPS Limited, a Macmillan Company.

Printed in Italy by Elcograf S.p.A.

The publisher has used its best endeavours to ensure that the website addresses
referred to in this book are correct and active at the time of going to press. However,
the publisher and the author have no responsibility for the websites and can make no
guarantee that a site will remain live or that the content will remain relevant, decent
or appropriate.

Hachette UK's policy is to use papers that are natural, renewable and recyclable
products and made from wood grown in sustainable forests. The logging and
manufacturing processes are expected to conform to the environmental regulations
of the country of origin.

Acknowledgements

My thanks are due to Mel Thompson for a very helpful review of the manuscript, to Charles Foster for reading it and describing it as 'antiseptic', to my cousin Peter Sobey for helping with proof-reading and to my wife Caroline and children Clare and Robert for trying to read the book, and being willing to discuss examples of crooked thought at the breakfast table.

I would particularly like to thank my late grandfather for asking me to carry on his work, and I hope that he would have approved of what has been done to his book.

Contents

Preface   vii

1 Different ways of using language   1

2 Words and facts   15

3 The meanings of words   29

4 Definition and some of its difficulties   37

5 Good and bad definitions   44

6 All and some   51

7 Some dishonest tricks in argument   62

8 Some logical fallacies   74

9 Habits of thought   85

10 Prejudice   97

11 Predigested thinking   111

12 Pitfalls in analogy   118

13 Oratory and suggestion   127

14 Tricks of suggestion   138

15 Straight thinking   146

16 The future of straight thinking   151

Appendix 1: Thirty-seven dishonest tricks commonly used in argument, with the methods of overcoming them   159

Appendix 2: A discussion illustrating crooked thinking   165

Index   171

Preface

The world's need for straight thinking and its susceptibility to crooked thinking are as great now as when my grandfather first wrote this book in the late 1920s. However, the relative importance of different kinds of abuse of language has changed, as has the political context in which they take place. For these reasons it seems a good idea to revise *Straight & Crooked Thinking* for the fifth time.

Although many books have been published with similar themes in the intervening years, this one has had an enduring appeal which makes it worth updating. A major part of this appeal is its emotional detachment and a dry sense of humour about the things that people do to language to obstruct clear thinking. I have attempted to retain these characteristics. By detachment I mean that, although it is made clear that straight thinking is preferable to crooked thinking, the message is not rammed down the reader's throat. As a result the book has the potential to be used for evil as well as good ends. It could just as well be used by a dishonest communicator to understand and refine his technique as by an honest person to understand how he is being duped by others.

It is important to remember that this book is a 'field guide', not a self-improvement manual. The features that make *Straight & Crooked Thinking* such an attractive book are a reflection of the humanity and intellectual independence of my grandfather. He was remarkable in his ability to write and talk in a detached and objective way even on issues about which he felt deeply.

Robert Thouless was born in Norwich in 1894. He was educated at a local grammar school and won an award to Corpus Christi College, Cambridge, where he studied physical sciences. During the First World War he served as a signals officer in the Salonika expeditionary force in northern Greece. He took part in a brief and unsuccessful British offensive against the Bulgarians, known as the Second Battle of Doiran. Robert was in the thick of this battle, and his diaries describe his experience of taking a telephone line through no-man's land towards the enemy lines. He continued in his task, despite shelling, gunfire and a dose of mustard gas.

After the war he returned to Cambridge, where he turned from the physical sciences to the emerging field of psychology. He was greatly influenced by his friend and colleague William Rivers, who is now best known for his work with shell-shocked patients (including the poet Siegfried Sassoon), during the First World War. Robert wrote his doctoral thesis on 'The Psychology of Religion'. This was published as a book which remained in print for nearly 60 years.

From 1921 to 1926 Robert was lecturer in psychology at the University of Manchester, where he met his future wife Priscilla Gorton, who was a lecturer in English. Between 1926 and 1938 he was head of the Department of Psychology at the University of Glasgow where he conducted some of the earliest experiments on visual perception, trying to understand the nature of optical illusions, and how they are seen differently by people of different cultural backgrounds. During this time he became interested in radio broadcasting, and two series of radio talks were turned into books. *The Control of the Mind* attracted little notice, but *Straight & Crooked Thinking* was immediately successful. It was deliberately written as a popular book because, as an academic psychologist, Robert Thouless thought that it was important for ordinary people to understand their unconscious impulses towards irrationality and how these irrational forces could be a major cause of war. The book was successful, perhaps partly because it presaged the rise of fascism in Europe and made comprehensible some of Hitler's tactics.

In 1938 Robert returned to Cambridge as a fellow of his old college and reader in the Department of Education. Although he had become a pacifist after the First World War, he recognized the need to fight against the Nazis and served in a Home Guard anti-aircraft battery. Ever the psychologist, he wrote notes about the morale of a small group of middle-aged and elderly men staying up night after night, sometimes in dreadful weather, without once catching sight of an enemy aircraft. *Straight & Crooked Thinking* was distributed to US troops during the Second World War, and a similar book with a more specialized theme, called *Straight Thinking in Wartime,* was published. This was based in part on a detailed analysis of Adolf Hitler's book *Mein Kampf*, and he was astonished by how little attention had been paid to how openly Hitler divulged his plans to gain power.

He remained at Cambridge for the rest of his life. He taught trainee teachers the basic principles of psychology, including the use of statistical methods. However, his research concentrated on visual perception and the paranormal. He was President of the British Psychological Society from 1949 to 50 and of the Society for Psychical Research from 1942 to 44. Although a frequent result of his painstaking investigations was the detection of cheating in apparent cases of psychic powers, he remained open to the possibility of such abilities. He was a close friend of the philosopher Ludwig Wittgenstein, and some of the ideas that he added to later editions of *Straight & Crooked Thinking* came from his discussions with Wittgenstein about the relationship between language and reality.

My grandfather retired shortly after I was born in 1960, but he continued to work, writing *Experimental Psychical Research* and *From Anecdote to Experiment in Psychical Research* as well as revising several of his earlier books. His last area of interest was the evidence for survival after death, and his last experiment (which required his death to carry it out) gained a certain degree of notoriety. He had become frustrated with the vagueness surrounding the supposed evidence for the dead communicating with the living, and tried to come up with a foolproof experiment. He devised a code that was unbreakable during his lifetime, with the intention of communicating the key through a medium after his death. The correct key would translate a coded message, and unlock a safe with a combination lock. About a hundred possible solutions were sent to the Society of Psychical Research by mediums, but none was right. Various suggestions were provided as to the reason for this, including the possibility that he had forgotten the key once he passed over to 'the other side'. However, given the reluctance of a number of **ix** mediums to return my telephone calls when I called asking for an appointment and giving my family name, I am inclined to a simpler explanation. Unfortunately the speed of improvement of computers outstripped that of psychic mediums, and the code was finally broken by a graduate student with a laptop only ten years after my grandfather's death, thus making 'Thouless's Last Experiment' redundant. However, it should be remembered that the test would only work if three conditions applied: that we survive bodily death, that the dead are able to communicate with the living, and finally (and most importantly) that they actually want to do so. Its failure says nothing about the possible truth of the first two conditions.

Since much of the value of *Straight & Crooked Thinking* has been its application of psychology and logic to current issues, it has been necessary to update it a number of times. New editions were brought out in 1953 and 1974. Interest was expressed in a further revision in the early 1980s, but my grandfather felt that since he was nearly ninety he was not sufficiently in touch with current politics and ideas to perform this task unaided. Therefore he asked me to help him. However, he died in 1984, before we could start work together on the project. Shortly before his death he asked me to continue without him. Although we did not have the chance to discuss detailed changes, we did talk about the general aim of the book and what sort of revision would be needed. I started this work during some enforced leisure time while I was under house arrest in China, and completed it while looking for the few surviving wildlife populations in the Saudi Arabian deserts. These experiences allowed me to source a number of examples for the book from my personal experiences. Apart from changing dated examples to more current ones, the major alteration was a restructuring of the chapters and their ordering.

Although in earlier editions the book had sold many hundreds of thousands of copies, the new edition came out in a small print run, and was not reprinted as the publisher was taken over by another company. Since copies were selling for up to $500 on Amazon, I thought that it was high time for a new edition 20 years later. The changes for this edition have been much fewer than for the last, and rather than trying to replace all outdated examples with modern ones, I have tried to provide a mixture of old and new to emphasize the point that this book is an 80-year-old classic that is still relevant today.

Although this is a book with two authors I have consistently used the first person singular to avoid distracting distinctions. It can more or less be assumed that references to events since the late 1970s are my experiences, while earlier ones have come from previous editions. When referring to people in general I have used the masculine personal pronoun where gender-neutral alternatives would be inelegant and distracting.

No doubt my personal political views, together with those of my grandfather, are apparent from the selection of examples, and I am no more impartial or immune to crooked thinking than any of my readers. I must apologize, but if a book such as this is to deal with controversial topics it is not possible to avoid some personal bias. In selecting topics for discussion I have necessarily chosen those which have struck me. It is always easier to find examples of crooked thinking in the words of one's opponents than in those of one's friends. The selection of material has necessarily been affected by differences between my interests and those of my grandfather. I cannot claim to approach my grandfather's knowledge or understanding in religious matters and for this reason they have received less emphasis than in earlier editions. My professional training is in ecology and animal behaviour, and most of my adult life has been spent working on wildlife conservation in Africa.

1

Different ways of using language

T HIS BOOK IS about the ways that people deceive others (and often themselves as well) by their use of language. By **straight thinking** I mean using language in an honest way to describe the world and how we feel about it: by **crooked thinking** I mean using language to manipulate people dishonestly or to obscure the true meaning of one's words. This may be deliberate or may result from confusion about how one is using language.

One of the ways in which confusion over use of language comes about is from uncertainty as to what we are doing in a particular act of communication or thinking. There are a number of different ways in which we can use language:

1 To give information, e.g. 'Kangaroos are found in Australia.' It is assumed that the listener already knows the meanings of the words 'kangaroos' and 'Australia', and is being given information about the connection between the facts that these two words represent.

2 To ask for information about a fact, e.g. 'Are there kangaroos in New Guinea?'

3 To indicate an emotional attitude, e.g. 'Kangaroos are horrid.'

4 To indicate how a word is used, by describing the relationship between an unknown or unfamiliar word and ones which are already known, e.g. '"Marsupials" are animals with pouches.'

5 To ask how a word is used, e.g. 'What is a "marsupial"?'
6 To get someone to carry out an action, e.g. 'Look at the kangaroo.'

These are, perhaps, the principal ways in which we use language, but there are also innumerable others, for example:

7 To make poetry.
8 To make a joke.
9 To make a quarrel.
10 To resolve a quarrel.
11 To give a greeting.

These are what the philosopher Wittgenstein has called different 'language games'. Confusions between these different ways of using language are encouraged by the fact that in any act of communication one may be playing several 'language games', or using language in more than one way, simultaneously. Someone may make a quarrel or write poetry, while at the same time indicating an emotional attitude or asking for information about a fact. 'To be or not to be, that is the question?' is a statement about a question, but it is also poetry.

There is a very common confusion between the first and third ways of using language, between statements of fact and indications of emotional attitude. When someone says 'Rover is a dog', he is stating a fact; he is employing the first of the ways of using language described above. If one of Rover's grandparents was a collie, another was an Irish terrier, another a fox terrier and the fourth a bulldog, these facts could be expressed by saying that he is a dog of mixed breed. Language would then still be used in the first manner of stating a fact. Suppose, however, that someone calls Rover a 'mongrel'. The matter is then more complicated. A word has been used that means the same as 'dog of mixed breed', but that may also arouse in its hearers an attitude of disapproval towards Rover. It may also, if used affectionately, arouse an attitude of approval. In either case the word 'mongrel' does not only indicate a fact, it also suggests an emotional attitude towards that fact; it combines the first and third ways of using language in the above list. The use of the word goes beyond mere factual description since the attitude of approval or disapproval that it suggests is some-

2 thing that belongs to the people discussing it and not to the dog that

is being discussed. Its master may think of it as a noble animal with a colourful ancestry but it is still a mongrel to his next-door-neighbour, particularly if he is a member of the Kennel Club and owns a pedigree bitch.

In the same way, an individual of African descent may be described as 'black', or with emotional disapproval and contempt as a 'nigger', a 'kaffir' or a 'coon'. The word 'black' is not technically more accurate than the other words since there are few Africans whose skin is actually black, rather than some shade of brown, and in any case the word 'nigger' is derived from the Latin for 'black'. However, 'black' is a word with a meaning that is generally understood and which is not felt to have particularly hostile or approving overtones. In Britain the word 'negro' was used as an objective term, while in America it was considered offensive, although it is also becoming less acceptable in Britain. In communication, what matters is how the other person interprets what you are saying, not what you think about it. You could say that it is perfectly acceptable to use words like 'yidd', 'dago' or 'kraut' because you do not have a hostile attitude to the people concerned, but other people will believe that you do have such an attitude because of your use of words.

When we become aware of this difference between the factual and emotional uses of words, we notice that words that carry more or less strong suggestions of emotional attitudes are very common, and are ordinarily used in the discussion of such controversial questions as those of politics, morals and religion. This is one reason why people can go on discussing such questions without getting much nearer to a rational solution of them.

There is a well-known saying that the word 'firm' can be declined as follows: I am **firm**, you are **obstinate**, he is **pig-headed**. This is a simple illustration of what is meant. 'Firm', 'obstinate' and 'pig-headed' all have the same factual meaning – that is, following one's own course of action and refusing to be influenced by other people's opinions. They have, however, different emotional meanings; 'firm' has an emotional meaning of approval, 'obstinate' of mild disapproval, 'pig-headed' of strong disapproval. If we wanted to find an emotionally neutral term that would convey the same idea without expressing either approval or disapproval, we should say perhaps 'X is not easily influenced'.

We can put this in another way. 'I am firm' is equivalent to saying 'I am not easily influenced and that is a good thing'; 'You are obstinate' is the same thing as 'You are not easily influenced and that is rather a bad thing'; 'He is pig-headed' means 'He is not easily influenced and that is a very bad thing.' We do not in ordinary conversation say explicitly whether we think the things we are talking about are good or bad; we can convey that by facial expression, by gesture or by the tone of our voice. In writing, we have none of these means of expressing our emotional attitude, but we still manage to avoid the necessity for saying 'This is a good thing' and 'That is a bad thing' by choosing words that imply opinions of goodness and badness, such as 'firm', 'obstinate', etc.

Such words are useful but they are a danger to reasonable thinking. A particular example that is widely used today is the word 'guerrilla'. One might decline this word in the following way: I am a *freedom fighter,* you are a *guerrilla,* he is a *terrorist.* All these words, as they are commonly used, have the same objective meaning. Groups such as the Tamil Tigers in Sri Lanka and the Taliban in Afghanistan have been described by all of these terms, according to the attitude of the person who is discussing them. It is generally accepted that freedom fighters are a good thing (because everyone approves of freedom) and should be supported, while terrorists are a bad thing (because most people reject the use of terror to achieve one's ends). Although these groups do differ importantly in their aims and methods, discussion of these differences can be severely prejudiced by referring to one group as 'heroic freedom fighters' and to another as a 'gang of bloodthirsty terrorists.'

On 17 September 2001 President George Bush said 'This crusade, this war on terrorism is going to take a while.' This statement caused a storm of protest around the world, and was a propaganda gift to Osama Bin Laden, who had been warning for years of crusader attacks on Islam. The word 'crusade' means different things to Christians and Muslims. In the Christian world its meanings have evolved well beyond the original meaning of someone who took up his cross to fight for Christianity, specifically to recover the holy city of Jerusalem. A crusade has now come to mean a vigorous action for a cause, with a strong overtone of approval. Usually crusaders are people who are dedicated to a worthwhile mission (although sometimes there is a hint that they are a bit over-enthusiastic). To people from the Muslim world, however, the word has none of these positive overtones, and a crusade is simply an attempt to conquer the holy lands of the Middle East. For them the crusaders are not well-meaning idealists but bloodthirsty outsiders who slaughtered innocents, sacked cities and cared nothing for the lives and culture of the people whose lands they conquered.

Similarly the word *jihad* is seen in different ways by different people. In the West it is often equated with the attacks on civilians by Al Quaeda and with a militant (and often anti-Western) form of Islam. To Muslims, however, 'jihad' has both violent and non-violent meanings. It can simply mean striving to live a moral and virtuous life, spreading and defending Islam as well as fighting injustice and oppression. Mahatma Gandhi's non-violent protests would be described in Arabic as 'jihad'.

In wartime we are particularly inclined to use words without thinking about their emotional content. We are naturally inclined to think well of our own soldiers and war aims and to disapprove of those of our enemies. We talk of the *spirit* of our soldiers and the *mentality* of the enemy soldiers, of the *heroism* of our own troops and the *fanaticism* of the enemy. When peace comes and we look back more objectively, we realize that a *spirit* and a *mentality* are factually the same, but one word has an emotional meaning of approval while the other expresses disapproval. We realize too that a soldier going forward under fire in extreme danger is doing the same thing whether he is one of our own soldiers or one of the enemy's, and that to distinguish between them by applying the word *fanaticism* to the action of one and *heroism* to that of the other is to misrepresent reality by using words to make an emotional distinction between two actions that are factually identical.

Such thinking in wartime may do much harm by leading ordinarily humane people to condone cruelty or even to perpetrate atrocities. The judgements implied by the use of a word may become part of the thought of the people who use it and make them act accordingly. Perhaps the most common example of this in wartime is the way that enemies are described as less than human so that the repugnance that people feel towards the killing of fellow-beings is reduced. To the **5**

German Nazis, the Russians, along with a number of other groups of people, were *untermensch* or subhumans; captured Russian soldiers were treated much more severely than the British, who were accorded the respect due to other human beings. Colonialists often meted out brutal treatment to the inhabitants of the countries they were occupying because they were only 'savages'.

A report was published in 1971 of an incident in Vietnam in which 24 women and children were shot by American soldiers. A technician trying to report the incident to his superiors was told: 'A gook is a gook. If it's got slanty eyes, kill the bastard.' The officer concerned justified his action by saying: 'They were enemy, not people.' While this kind of misuse of language is unlikely to be the sole cause of such incidents, it cannot but have an effect on the behaviour of the people who use it.

Another way of overcoming the natural reluctance of most soldiers to kill other people is to use words to describe the act of killing which have the effect of distancing the user from the reality of the act. Phrases such as *extreme prejudice*, *special treatment* and *final solution* sound more technical and have less emotional impact than the word *kill*. *Extermination* implies that the victims are vermin whom it is one's duty to destroy. Often the same act may be described by one side as an *execution* – implying legality and justice – and by the other as *murder*.

Emotionally tinged words are also used in political discussion. A proposed measure that is likely to meet with general public approval is *popular* and shows that the government of the day is *caring* and concerned to fulfil the wishes of the electorate in a truly democratic manner. The opposition will dismiss the same measure as *electioneering* by an administration that is trying to achieve its cynical ends by hoodwinking the people. Those who show enthusiasm for proposals with which a speaker disagrees are *extremists*, while those showing similar enthusiasm on his own side are called *staunch*.

Thinking on religious questions is also often made difficult by the use of emotionally toned words. Thus a man who holds firmly a definite system of religious beliefs may be called a *bigot* by those who disapprove of him and a *man of faith* by those who approve of him. *Strong in the faith of our fathers* and *shackled by an outworn creed* are phrases

which may have identical factual meanings but opposite emotional meanings. The emotional meaning of each of them confuses thought by directing attention away from the point that, in order to decide whether we ought to hold a body of beliefs, we have to consider only whether they are true; the fact that they were believed by people in the past is not in itself a sufficient reason for holding them and is a still worse reason for rejecting them.

In criticism of pictures and books we may also find interference with exact thinking by the use of emotional language. Many years ago, when such subjects were less freely discussed than they are now, a woman novelist, Radclyffe Hall, wrote a book called *The Well of Loneliness* about lesbianism. This was attacked in a newspaper article in the following words: 'Its vicious plea for the acknowledgement and condonation of sexual perversity and the grounds on which it is based, loosen the very sheet-anchor of conduct.' This passage calls out such strong emotions of abhorrence that most readers would have been content to condemn the novel without further inquiry. Yet the effect is gained entirely by the choice of words with emotional meanings. It happens to deal with a subject on which emotions were strong, so a dispassionate examination was all the more necessary. We note that the word *plea* means simply an argument, plus a suggestion of repugnance for the kind of argument used, that *condonation* is tolerance plus an emotional suggestion that such tolerance is indefensible, that *sexual perversity* is a minority sexual practice plus an emotional suggestion of abhorrence. The *loosening of a sheet-anchor* is a metaphor implying change and suggesting to a landsman the emotion of fear, while *conduct* is used as if it meant behaviour of which we approve!

So reducing to its bare bones of objective fact (ignoring for a moment the special difficulties raised by the word *vicious*) the passage becomes: 'Its argument for the acknowledgement and tolerance of unusualness in sexual practice, and the grounds on which it is based, change the principles of behaviour.' This is clearly an important statement if it is true, but is not enough in itself to condemn the book, because undoubtedly our principles of behaviour do need changing from time to time. We can only decide intelligently whether or not they need changing in this particular case when we have made a dispassionate examination of what the proposed changes are and why they are defended. As in all other cases, discussion of the question **7** with emotionally charged words obscures the problem and makes a sensible decision difficult or impossible.

The word *vicious* has some special difficulties of its own. Certainly this word has an emotional meaning of strong disapproval, but in this case we cannot replace it with an emotionally neutral word which has the same factual meaning since no such word exists. If we want to express the same meaning, we can call the book 'bad', 'corrupt' or 'evil', but whatever word we choose will have the same emotional meaning of disapproval. Can we then say that such words should not be used since they do not state facts but are only used to arouse emotion?

This is a problem about which there has been much dispute. Some philosophers have maintained that all such words as 'vicious', 'bad', 'good', 'beautiful' and 'ugly' only indicate the speaker's own emotional reactions towards certain actions and things, and not properties of those actions and things themselves. But when we see someone carry out a mean or selfish action and say that his action is 'bad', we certainly intend to say something about the action itself and not merely about how we feel about it. This is clear from the fact that it makes sense to say, 'I think swearing is bad although I don't find it offensive', just as it makes sense to say, 'That picture is, no doubt, good although I don't happen to like it myself.' So when we call a book 'vicious' we are saying something about the book rather than just about our own feelings, but in order to give objective meaning to the use of such a word we would need to specify why we call it 'vicious'. This might be stated in terms of its expected impact on readers, or on the motivation of its author.

If, however, we agree that the statement that a book is vicious has a meaning which is not merely emotional, we must also agree that it is not quite the same kind of meaning as a simple statement of fact such as 'This is a book.' Whether the book is good or bad is a real question, but it is a question that is peculiarly difficult to decide. Our own statement one way or the other is likely to be nothing but a reflection of our own personal prejudices and to have, therefore, no sort of exactness. At the same time, such words certainly arouse strong emotions and should, therefore, be used sparingly in honest argument. The use of words implying moral judgements in the course of argument is usually an attempt to distort the hearers' view of the truth by arousing

emotions.

If we are trying to decide a simple question of fact, such words should be left out, because it is easier to settle one question at a time. If a man is accused of poisoning his wife the prosecuting attorney should not say, 'This scoundrel who hounded his wife to her grave.' The question to be decided is whether the man did poison his wife. If he did, he is almost certainly a scoundrel, but calling him a scoundrel does not help to decide the question of fact. On the contrary, it makes a correct decision more difficult by arousing emotions of hatred for the accused in the minds of the jury. Another obvious objection to the use of the word 'scoundrel' before the man is convicted, which puts it in the ranks of 'crooked thinking', is that it 'begs the question' or assumes what is yet to be proved. The man is only shown to be a scoundrel if he is guilty, and yet the word has been used in the course of an argument to prove that he is guilty.

These two objections can be urged against the word 'vicious' in the condemnation of a book quoted above. It calls up strong emotions, making a just decision of the nature of the book difficult, and it assumes exactly what the article professes to prove, that the book was a bad one.

The use of emotionally toned words is not, of course, always to be condemned. It is always harmful when the situation is one which requires that factual information should be communicated or that people should be enabled to think clearly so that they may decide on a disputed factual matter. In poetry, on the other hand, emotional language has a proper place because in poetry (as in some kinds of prose) the arousing of various emotions may be an important part of the purpose for which the words are used.

In 'The Eve of St Agnes' Keats has written:

> Full on this casement shone the wintry moon
> And threw warm gules on Madeline's fair breast.

These are beautiful lines. Let us notice how much of their beauty follows from the proper choice of emotionally coloured words and how completely it is lost if these words are replaced by neutral ones. The words with strikingly emotional meanings are *casement*, *gules*, *Madeline*, *fair* and *breast*. *Casement* means simply a kind of window with emotional associations because it is old-fashioned and in this **9** case has coloured glass in it through which the moon is shining. *Gules* is the heraldic term for red, with the suggestion of romance which accompanies all heraldry. *Madeline* is simply a girl's name, but one which is uncommon today. *Fair* means, in fact, that her skin was white or uncoloured – a necessary condition if the colours of the window are to show up – but also *fair* has overtones of attractiveness. *Breast* has similar emotional meanings, and the aim of simple description might have been equally well attained if it had been replaced by a neutral word such as 'chest'.

Let us now try the experiment of keeping these two lines in a metrical form, but replacing all the emotionally coloured words by others that are as emotionally neutral as possible while conveying the same factual meaning. We may, for example, write:

> Full on this window shone the wintry moon,
> Making red marks on Jane's uncoloured chest.

No one will doubt that all of its poetic value has been knocked out of the passage by these changes. Yet the lines still have the same factual meaning; it is only the emotional meaning that has been destroyed.

Now if Keats had been writing a scientific description for a textbook on physics instead of a poem, it would have been necessary for him to have used some such coldly objective terms as those into which we have just translated his lines. Such emotionally charged phrases as *warm gules* and *fair breast* would only have obscured the facts to which the scientist exactly but unbeautifully refers when he speaks of 'the selective transmission of light by pigmented glass.'

Nor is it reasonable to condemn all use of emotionally charged words in ordinary conversation. Conversation would be dull if it did not include indications of how the speaker felt about the things he was talking about. These indications are provided in various ways, partly by the use of emotionally charged words, partly by changes in intonation. No one would wish to eliminate this factor in conversation, although one may have doubts about its usefulness in public discussion.

Even emotional oratory has its place. I would suggest, however, that this place is not where it is often found – as a technique of persuasion when a responsible decision is to be made. It may, on the other

10

hand, be an invaluable stimulus to action when what is required is to persuade people to do something which it is already agreed is right or at least necessary. So one may justify the emotional oratory of Winston Churchill during the Second World War. Then the situation required people to endure hardship and to take action necessary for survival. There was already general agreement that this action should be taken. As John F. Kennedy's speech writer Theodore Sorensen said: 'The right speech on the right topic, delivered by the right speaker in the right way at the right moment can ignite a fire, change men's minds, open their eyes, alter their votes, bring hope to their lives, and, in all these ways, change the world.'

The same sort of oratory is less useful in time of peace when what is required is that people shall make responsible decisions as to what is to be done. Effective democracy requires that people shall make decisions by a process of calm appraisal of the facts. Such calm appraisal is obstructed by the use of emotional oratory in presentation of the facts. After the decision, action follows, and into that action may be put all the emotion which, in an ideal democracy, has been excluded from the preliminary process of decision-making.

The psychological purpose of emotion (anger, fear, benevolence, etc.) is to make people act effectively. It muddles thought but it stimulates action. The ideal is to think calmly and to act effectively. We should think calmly and factually about such things as poverty, oppression of minorities, war, unrestricted population growth, and environmental damage. If we decide calmly and rationally that these are great evils which may be overcome by our efforts, then we may usefully put all the passion of which we are capable into action directed towards overcoming them.

An important part of the development of modern science has been the process of making less use of terms conveying emotional attitudes and more of those that unemotionally indicate objective facts. It was not always so. The old alchemists called gold and silver 'noble' metals, and thought that this emotionally coloured word indicated something belonging to the metals themselves from which their properties could be deduced. Other metals were called 'base'. Although these terms have survived as convenient labels for the modern chemist they carry none of their old emotional significance.

In popular discussion, on the other hand, such words are still used with their full emotional meaning, as when the 'nobility' of man is contrasted with his alleged 'base' origin. In some branches of biology, particularly in the study of behaviour, words are used which have not been fully divorced from their emotional meanings. Arguments may be generated by the confusion between a term used in its objective sense and the same word which is used by laymen with a strong emotional content. This is particularly likely where a scientific term has been adopted in common speech or where a common word has been taken up and redefined by scientists. Words describing human behaviour such as 'rape', 'incest', 'adultery' and 'infanticide' – which have strong emotional overtones resulting from implicit moral feelings – are used to describe similar behaviour shown by animals, and are often given more precise definitions.

Emotional oratory, as has already been pointed out, has its legitimate place. If there is no doubt about what we ought to do, then emotional oratory may be properly used to stir us to do it. Such oratory is out of place when the problem before us is to make a decision, as in a political election. The theory of democracy is that in an election the people have to make a rational decision. If they had to be stirred to do something arduous and distasteful (as in a war or revolution) then emotional oratory would be a useful means of getting them to do it. Since what they are required to do in an election is to think clearly and come to a sensible decision, the use of emotional language by political speakers is altogether to be condemned, since it makes clear thinking and sensible decisions more difficult.

However, political speakers are more interested in creating conviction than in promoting clear thinking, so they will go on using emotional language. Nothing that we can say will stop them. On the other hand, we can educate ourselves in such a way as to make us relatively immune to the influence of such language if we become aware of what is being done and, instead of responding with the emotions that the speaker intends, think of the factual meaning of what he is saying and discount its emotional meaning.

So that we may become able to do this, I suggest that we should try to do some practical work on the subject of this chapter instead of being content merely to read it. If you were studying botany, you would not only read books on botany, you would gather plants from the hedges and weeds from your garden, dissect them, examine them with a microscope, and draw them in your notebook. Psychology, too, should be studied by practical methods. Emotional thinking is to be found in the leading articles of newspapers, in the words of people discussing political, religious or moral questions, and in the speeches made by public figures when these deal with controversial matters. In order to understand it, we should collect specimens for study and dissection.

The practical exercise which I recommend is one that I have already performed on some passages in which truth seemed to be obscured by emotional thinking. I suggest that readers should copy out controversial passages from newspapers, books or speeches that contain emotionally coloured words. Then they should underline all the emotional words, afterwards rewriting the passages with the emotional words replaced by neutral ones. Examine the passage then in its new form in which it merely states facts without indicating the writer's emotional attitude towards them, and see whether it is still good evidence for the proposition it is trying to prove. If it is, the passage is a piece of straight thinking in which emotionally coloured words have been introduced merely as an ornament. If not, it is crooked thinking because the conclusion depends not on the factual meaning of the passage but on the emotions aroused by the words.

When we condemn the ill-considered use of emotional words in writings and speeches, we must remember that this is a symptom of a more deep-seated evil – their prevalence in our own private, unexpressed thinking. Many of our political speakers whose speeches stir us as we are stirred by romantic poetry show themselves unable to think calmly and objectively on any subject. They have so accustomed themselves to think in emotionally toned words that they can no longer think in any other way. They should have been poets or actors, but certainly not statesmen.

We can best guard against being misled by emotional oratory by making sure that our own minds do not get into such a state. It is not that we should never use emotional words in our thinking but that we should know when we are doing so, and have a method of counteracting their effects. When we catch ourselves thinking in emotional 13 terms, let us form a habit of translating our thoughts into emotionally neutral words. So we can save ourselves from ever being so enslaved by emotional words and phrases that they prevent us from thinking objectively when we need to do so – that is, whenever we have to come to a decision on any debatable matter.

In the same way, I suggest that those who wish to learn more of the nature of crooked thinking should, after reading each of the following chapters, try to collect specimens of the tricks described from the sources I have mentioned. In some cases I shall suggest practical operations which can be carried out on them in order to make clear the nature of the crooked thinking (as, for example, in Chapter 9 in the provision of a new setting for doubtful propositions which run along the lines of your own thought habits). In this way it will be possible to gain a better mastery of the subject and a better protection against your own intellectual exploitation by unscrupulous writers.

The intention of this book is primarily practical. Its main purpose is not to stimulate intellectual curiosity but to increase awareness of the processes of crooked thinking and crooked communication and to provide safeguards against these. It would not have succeeded in its object if it merely led its readers to study books about logic. The test of its success is rather whether it makes it less easy for one of its readers to be persuaded by a salesman to buy a vacuum cleaner or an encyclopaedia that he or she does not want, and less easy for a political speaker to influence his or her way of voting by such irrational means as the use of emotional language or confident affirmation. More importantly, I hope that it will make it less easy for the reader to hate the 'enemy', whoever they may be at the moment, 'commie', 'jihadi' or 'Paki', with that blind lack of understanding that comes from the various emotional ways of thinking about them.

2

Words and facts

IF SPIES WANT to send secret messages when they know that enemies are tapping their telephones and opening their mail, they may use a simple kind of code. A postcard saying 'The weather is lovely' may actually mean 'I have assassinated the president'; or 'Wish you were here' may mean 'There are 25 submarines in harbour.' In both cases, the real message has no apparent connection with what is written; the person who receives it will only understand the true meaning if he or she has the correct key, which may be a book in which they can look up 'The weather is lovely' to find out what it really means. Anyone else, even if he is suspicious (perhaps because it is raining), will be none the wiser.

Codes can be much more elaborate than this. Some substitute letters or numbers for each letter in the original, while others have a complicated system in which each letter is represented by a different one each time that it appears. The code does not have to be in letters and numbers; it could be in the arrangement of notes in a piece of music or in the colour of one's clothes. What codes have in common is that they use abstract symbols, such as letters, numbers or colours, to represent a message. In order to interpret these symbols you must have a key to the code – a key which will unlock the message. With it you can understand what is being said, and reconstruct exactly the original message. Without it, the symbols will be no more than a meaningless jumble.

Language itself is a kind of code. We use words, and the way that they are put together, as symbols to represent the world and **15** our thoughts about it. The key is the way we have learned to use the words, and perhaps some basics of grammar that are built into the circuitry of our brains. The fact that language is a code becomes apparent when you think of two people describing the same object in different languages. What they are saying has the same meaning, but if they cannot understand each other's language the sounds will be incomprehensible. It is as if they were trying to interpret a coded message using the wrong key.

There are some important differences between language and other codes. In simple codes each part of the coded message translates directly and uniquely back into the original message, using the correct key. This is possible because, in codes depending on substitution of letters, there are only 26 possibilities to deal with. In codes that substitute words or whole sentences, then there are still a limited number of alternatives to be considered. However, there are so many different objects and ideas in the world that we cannot attach a unique label to each one. Instead we put them together in categories of objects or ideas and give them the same name. This process of *classification* is one of the most important attributes of language and many of the problems of correct usage of language are connected with it.

Another major difference between language and simple codes is that there is no written code book. Dictionaries do enable us to find the meanings of new words, but it would be very difficult to learn to use language just by using a dictionary. In order for a dictionary to be useful we need to have an understanding of the structure of language and to know the words that are being used to define other words.

Ambiguities that arise out of the complex structure of language can be illustrated by the difficulty that people have in programming computers to understand English. A computer can become hopelessly stuck over difficulties that we are not even aware of. Pairs of sentences such as 'The bishop was drunk' and 'The water was drunk'; or 'I shot the white rabbit with a gun' and 'I saw the white rabbit with pink eyes' have meanings that are difficult for a computer to distinguish, yet for a human the differences are very clear. Understanding the meanings of words by their context is a skill that can only be acquired by experience, rather than by using a dictionary, and this is a very important

part of the decoding process.

Learning to use language is a task of great complexity, but we are able to do it without worrying about the nature of language and its relationship to what it is being used to describe. If we have never paused to consider how to define a table, we may forget that the word 'table' is merely a convenient label for a class of similar flat-topped objects with legs, and has no meaning in itself. We may also forget that, although the words 'beauty' and 'truth' can be used as easily as the word 'table', this does not indicate anything about their meaning, or lack of it. In the next four chapters we will discuss problems to do with words and their relationship to what they are used to describe. The first problem is the confusion between arguments about words and arguments about the facts that they describe.

In one of his books, the American psychologist and philosopher William James tells a story of how, during a camping holiday, he returned from a solitary walk to find the rest of his party engaged in a furious argument. The problem was this. Suppose that a squirrel is on one side of a tree-trunk and a man is on the other side. The man starts going around the tree but however fast he goes round, the squirrel goes around in the same direction, so that he is always facing the man by keeping the trunk of the tree between the man and himself. The question at the heart of the argument was whether the man went around the squirrel or not. The party was evenly divided, and it is not surprising that they had argued for a long time without coming any closer to a solution. They appealed to James, who replied that it was not a question of fact, but of words, of how one is to use the words 'go around'.

This is a trivial example of a very important type of dispute, in which the question at issue cannot be resolved because both sides treat a problem of words as a problem of fact. No question of fact divided the people arguing about the squirrel. Both sides accepted that the man was circling around the tree to which the squirrel was clinging and also that the squirrel was facing him the whole time. Those who said that the man went around the squirrel pointed out that he was first to the north of the squirrel, then to the west of it, then to the south, then to the north again, and so on. But this fact was not disputed by their opponents. Those who said the man did not go around the squirrel pointed out that he was not successively to the front of it, **17** then to the side of it, then to the back of it, etc. Again this fact was not disputed by the other side. Indeed, no question of fact divided them. The only question was which of these sets of facts should be described by the words 'go around'.

Usually when the phrase 'going around' is used, it refers to a stationary object. In this case 'going around' implies that the movements of the subject describe a circle or some other closed shape around the object, and that during the course of this movement the subject would have been able to see the entire circumference of the object. Under most circumstances in which the phrase is used, both of these conditions will be satisfied. It is only in cases such as the one described above, or perhaps when someone is circling a merry-go-round at exactly the same speed that it itself is rotating, that one of these conditions is not met and it becomes unclear whether the phrase 'going around' describes the situation correctly.

This particular verbal problem could not have been settled even if James's friends had argued for ever. Plainly it could not, in this case, be settled by an appeal to a dictionary, since no dictionary would be found to define 'going around' so precisely as to distinguish between these two possible uses of the words. Nor could it be settled by argument, since one has a perfect right to use the words 'going around' in whichever of the two ways one likes. If indeed the disputants had appreciated that their difference was a purely verbal one they would have stopped arguing, since they would have realized that it could not be settled. The important character of the dispute was that it was a verbal problem discussed as if it were a factual one.

Many discussions are of this type, and it is failure to understand their verbal nature that leads to much pointless argument. Children may have serious disputes about whether tomatoes are fruits or not. No question of fact is involved; the question is the verbal one of how one is to use the word 'fruit'. If we follow botanists in defining it as the part of a plant which encloses the seed, tomatoes are fruits. If, however, we consider that fruits are plant parts that are either naturally sweet or sweetened with sugar and eaten for dessert or at breakfast, then tomatoes are not fruits (but rhubarb is). You are entitled to use the word 'fruit' in either way. In the rather unlikely event of a botanist getting involved in the dispute and saying that theirs is the correct way of using the word, you may point out that the other is also a present-day use; it may even be an older one. No one would, however, be much interested in arguing the question if they realized that it was only a question of how a word was to be used; what gives liveliness to the discussion is the mistaken idea that it is a question of fact.

Later in life, we may become trapped in the same kind of dispute when we discuss whether discrimination in favour of racial minorities in the provision of jobs or housing is a form of racism or not. One side may say that it is racist because it involves treating people differently according to their racial background; the other may say that it is not, because it is only by these means that we can help members of minority groups to reach equality with the rest of the population. Again, this is a verbal question, of whether we are to use the word 'racism' to mean treating minority groups badly or to mean treating them differently from other people. Unfortunately, this kind of dispute is widespread. People fight over the meanings of powerfully emotive words in much the same manner that soldiers on Napoleonic battlefields fought over regimental standards. Just as 'losing the colours' may have been more important than losing the battle, winning the right to use a word in the way you want may be more important than winning the real argument.

In many cases the verbal and factual elements are mixed together, and it may be difficult to disentangle the verbal aspect of the problem. Opponents and supporters of nuclear weapons often argue about whether particular kinds of weapons are 'defensive' or not. Some people would say that you cannot under any circumstances call a weapon with the capacity to kill millions of people 'defensive'. A general might say that it is battlefield nuclear weapons – bombs or shells with limited range and destructive capacity – which are truly defensive because they cannot be used to attack an enemy's cities, but are designed to halt him once he has already launched an attack. Other people might say that, on the contrary, it is the intercontinental ballistic missiles, the ones with the capacity to destroy whole cities and to strike to the heart of the enemy's country, that are 'defensive', because what prevents the enemy from attacking in the first place is fear of these weapons. Some politicians might say that all their nuclear weapons are defensive, because they would never consider using them in an aggressive way. **19**

It is unlikely that people arguing about this issue would welcome the intervention of someone who pointed out that the question was primarily a verbal one as to how the word 'defence' was to be defined. The most obvious definition is the use of force designed to stop an enemy in his tracks once he has already launched an attack. Although military planners might consider that some kinds of nuclear weapons are to be used 'defensively' in this sense of the word, such a policy would result in the defending side being the first one to use nuclear force. Politicians therefore tend to describe the weapons as defensive in another way. They are defensive because they are a deterrent – they frighten the enemy so that he will not attack in the first place. According to one version of this argument, the deterrent power of small nuclear weapons is greater, since their use would be easier to contemplate than that of intercontinental ballistic missiles, which would provoke instant and massive retaliation. This version of 'defence' depends on so convincing your enemies of your willingness to use the weapons that they will never actually need to be used. A third way of using the word 'defence' is to mean attacking the enemy before he has a chance to attack you. This may seem ridiculous but it is worth remembering that 'self-defence' has been invoked by the aggressor in almost every war of modern times.

One reason why none of the disputants in this sort of argument would welcome such a solution is that they would all feel that there was a real difference between them that was not just verbal. Of course there is, but this is only obscured by the confusion between words and facts that results from discussing the problem as if it were purely factual. The real difference is whether one thinks that a particular 'defence policy' will be effective or foolhardy. If you believe, for instance, that the result of having nuclear weapons will be the likely destruction of civilization in a nuclear war, you are hardly likely to describe such weapons as defensive.

There is another difference – one of moral valuation – which is very unlikely to be removed by argument. By 'valuation' we mean such questions as whether a thing is bad or good, beautiful or ugly. The best we can do in such a case is to disentangle what part of our difference of opinion is merely a difference in the use of words, and **20** then to see what difference remains as to fact or valuation. Once any differences as to interpretation of facts have been established, then one can at least agree to differ as to the moral valuation, which in this case is whether nuclear weapons are intrinsically 'evil' or whether they are neutral objects with the capacity to be 'good' or 'evil' depending on what use we put them to. Even though the argument will not have been settled, and probably never can be while people hold different views of morality, at least we will be clearer about our own position and that of our opponents.

The reason why so much time is spent in this kind of dispute is that people are unwilling or unable to separate the verbal, factual and moral strands of their argument. This confusion is perhaps less the result of dishonesty than lack of skill in the use of language and a reluctance to see things objectively, when strong emotional issues are involved.

There is a method of trying to use a verbal proposition to settle a question of fact which is perhaps worth noting. This is the use of a tautology – a statement such as 'a cow is a cow', in which the same thing is said twice. If someone came up to you and said 'A cow is a cow', you would probably not be impressed, because he would not have told you very much. However, tautologies are often used in a concealed way, so that it is not immediately obvious that the two parts of the statement say the same thing.

A form of tautology which is frequently used in arguments can be illustrated by the following example. Suppose that two teachers, Mr Smith and Mr Brown, are discussing the merits of different kinds of schooling. Mr Brown is an enthusiast for stern discipline and traditional methods; Mr Smith advocates a more liberal approach, with pupils being given more freedom. At some stage of the argument Mr Brown says: 'You must admit that too much freedom in schools is a bad thing.' Mr Smith is put in a difficult position. He is asked to deny something that he cannot reasonably deny. He cannot deny it because it is a purely verbal argument, since it says nothing factual at all. The meaning of 'too much' is 'a quantity so great that it is a bad thing.' This means that the statement that 'too much freedom in schools is a bad thing' is tautologous. Of course it might be that Mr Smith does not actually consider that there is any amount of freedom which could be too great. In this case he still would not be able to disagree with the **21** original statement, but he could say that it was inappropriate, since 'too much freedom' is not possible; it is not that it is a bad thing, but that it cannot exist.

It is likely, however, that he would be unwilling to defend such an extreme position as this. He is only prepared to argue that there should be a great deal more freedom in schools than Mr Brown would allow. He can point out the tautological nature of Mr Brown's statement in some such way as: 'Of course, too much of anything is a bad thing.' Then he can bring back the discussion to the real point at issue, saying perhaps: 'But what I should consider the right amount of freedom is what you would call "too much".' Even so, if the discussion took place before an uncritical audience, Mr Brown might unfairly have gained an advantage.

An argument of this kind is wrong, no matter what the subject matter is. Mr Smith's statement that 'Too much flogging in schools is a bad thing', is just as dishonest.

Another, more subtle kind of tautology is used in arguments where the truth of a statement is implied by the way in which language is used. For example, it used to be argued that the soul was something independent of the body and that it must, therefore, survive physical death. The proper way of stating this argument would be that we use the word 'soul' as if it were a thing which existed apart from the body, and that this use of language leads us to believe that there is something which will survive the death of the body. It then becomes clear that this is a speculative argument based on our use of language. The conclusion, of course, may be true or false, but the argument itself gives no sound reason for saying that the conclusion is true.

Now one is more likely to hear this argument put the other way round. It has been suggested that there is no problem in understanding the phenomenon of consciousness, since the idea of the conscious mind as something separate from the brain is a mistake in the use of language. We know that we think, but it is a linguistic mistake to attribute this to something called the mind, rather than to the brain. This is an equally speculative argument. It also tries to draw a conclusion about facts by the study of language.

In both cases the answer is that we must make our language fit the observed facts and not try to draw conclusions as to the facts from our use of language. If we are convinced that nothing survives our death, then we do not need the word 'soul' or 'spirit' in our vocabulary (unless, of course, we need it to cover some other fact). If, however, we think that we have some reason for believing that we will survive the death of our body, then we shall need some such noun as 'soul' or 'spirit' to describe what survives. In either case our use of language must be determined by what appear to be the facts. We are guilty of crooked thought if we let our belief about facts be determined by our previous use of language.

Let us pause at this point to make clear the use of a convention that is generally adopted and which is very useful for avoiding confusion between words and facts. It is that of enclosing a word between single inverted commas when we are referring to the word itself and omitting the commas when we are talking about the thing the word stands for. Thus a verbal dispute will be about 'democracy' while a factual dispute may be about democracy, that is, about the systems of government for which the word 'democracy' stands. If we think that we are discussing democracy when the question at issue is really about 'democracy', then we are mistaking a verbal for a factual dispute.

On the other hand, it is worth noting that in a written piece the use of inverted commas around a word can be an effective trick to throw doubt on somebody's credentials or beliefs. '"Doctor" Smith, that well-known "honest politician"' is clearly thought by the writer to be neither a doctor nor an honest politician, but nowhere has the doubt been explicitly stated. This is a particularly dubious trick since the writer can cast aspersions on someone without having to take the consequences of doing so.

We can consider how verbal problems arise and how they come to be mistaken for factual problems in another way. Suppose that someone said that he was going to use the symbol '9' for the first number, '8' for the next number, '7' for the number after that, and '2' for the number after that. It would be no good telling him that this was wrong; he would reply that he was living in a free country and could use symbols as he liked. Some of the arithmetical statements he would make would look very odd, such as '8 times 8 is 2'. We might at first suppose that he has produced a new and extraordinary way of doing arithmetic. But this would be wrong; it would be the **23** old arithmetic expressed in a new system of symbols. What he meant by '8 times 8 is 2' would be exactly the same as we mean by '2 times 2 is 4'. He would, in effect, have made the same factual statement using a different code. There would be obvious objections to what was proposed; it would serve no useful purpose and it would be inconvenient. Its adoption would not enable us to say anything new, and it would lead to much misunderstanding.

Of course, there might be a point in the use of new symbolism. Mathematicians do sometimes use the symbols '10' for the number after 1, '11' for the next number, '100' for the next number, and so on. This is called 'expressing the numbers in binary' or 'in the scale of two'. Then the mathematician might say '11 times 11 is 1001' and mean exactly the same as we mean by '3 times 3 is 9'. This symbolism is convenient for some purposes, such as working with computers, or counting on your thumbs, but it does not enable the mathematician to say anything new, and if he used this notation in a context in which the ordinary number symbols would be expected, he would have to explain what he was doing if he did not want to be misunderstood.

This may all seem obvious when we are talking about numbers; it is often overlooked when similar situations occur in the use of words. Suppose someone says: 'Democracy is not government by the people, but the willing agreement of the people to a system of laws imposed on them by their rulers.' He is not announcing some new and previously unknown fact about democracy; he is simply telling us that he is going to use the word 'democracy' in a way different from that of most other people.

There may be some point in his wish to use the word in a different way but, whether there is or not, endless confusion can result from failure to realize that that is what he is doing. He will use sentences different from those of other people when they are saying the same thing. He may say, for example, 'Germany under Hitler was a true democracy' while someone else may say, 'Hitler destroyed democracy in Germany.' There would be no difference of fact between these two statements, any more than there is between '3 times 3 is 9' in the ordinary use of numbers and '11 times 11 is 1001' when we are using the

scale of two. This is obviously the case when we put the statements in an expanded form. 'Germany under Hitler was a country in which there was a willing agreement of the people to laws imposed on them by their rulers' is perfectly consistent with the statement that 'Hitler destroyed government by the people in Germany.' They are different statements, both of which may be true. They only appear to contradict each other when they are made with the word 'democracy' used with one meaning in one of them and with another meaning in the other.

To argue about which of the two is the true statement without noticing that the difference lies in the use of words is another example of mistaking a verbal difference for a factual one. Of course the man who makes the statements about democracy being the willing agreement of people to laws imposed on them by their rulers is likely to invite this confusion by regarding himself as making a statement of fact and not an announcement of how he is going to use words. He may even make this confusion inevitable by claiming to have discovered the fact he thinks he is announcing. He may say, for example, that as a result of the study of Roman history or of having paid a visit to Cuba, he has learned that democracy is really the willing agreement of the people to laws imposed on them from above. This is nonsense. No study of non-verbal facts can tell him how to use a word. His studies and visits may convince him that the agreement of people to laws imposed on them is an important thing and, therefore, one that we should distinguish in words. They may convince him that it is a better thing than people making laws for themselves. But they cannot possibly tell him that the word 'democracy' has to be used for it. That is his own choice; he may bring arguments in its favour, but he cannot claim that the choice was forced on him by the facts.

The next stage of the dispute is likely to be the somewhat unprofitable one of whether this is the right use of the word 'democracy'. His opponent may say 'Of course, you can use words in your way and we will try to understand you, but what "democracy" really means is government by the people.' This is better than discussing 'what democracy really is', because it puts the difference at the right point, as a difference about the word, not as a difference about a fact.

Yet it is not a profitable thing to discuss. Not because there is no question as to the right use of a word, but because there are several **25** different questions, all fairly easy to decide if they are separated out, but likely to lead to interminable dispute if they are confused together under the one question of the right use of the word.

The first question is, what was the original meaning of the word. Very often the words we are likely to argue about have Greek, Latin or Anglo-Saxon origins, and a good etymological dictionary will tell us what these are and what they meant. For example, 'democracy' comes from the Greek *demos* meaning 'people', and *kratos,* the verb 'to rule'. So its etymological meaning is 'rule by the people'. This does not help us much, since it does not say how the people are to rule, whether they make political decisions or formulate laws themselves, or whether they choose representatives to do it for them, and if so, what system they use for making this choice.

When people are disputing about the right use of a word, they are not likely to appeal to an etymological dictionary, which tells them about its Greek or Latin origin. They are more likely to claim that their sense of the word is the one in which it is ordinarily used. This certainly is a more important question. The ways in which words are used change in the course of time, and the origins of words are not always indications of how they are used now. The question of how a word is used now is more important than its original meaning, but it is much less easy to decide. It may seem that we can turn to a dictionary to find out how a word is used now, but the kinds of words we are likely to be disputing about are used in many different ways. The better the dictionary, the more uses of a word it will give. The Oxford English Dictionary lists four main meanings of the word 'democracy' and that falls far short of the real variety of its meanings. If you examined books by different authors, it would probably not be difficult to find 20 different ways in which 'democracy' is used. So if someone says he wants to use the word in a new way, he is only increasing a diversity which is already large.

We cannot reasonably try to stop him from using words in a new way by urging that they have a single clearly defined meaning from which it would be wrong to depart; this is very often not the case. If, however, the meaning he proposes is neither the original etymological meaning nor any of the currently accepted meanings, it is reasonable

to point out that a new use adds to the confusion that already exists.

But our complaint is that the new use is inconvenient rather than that it is wrong. If the person proposing the new use is willing to put up with the inconvenience of being very generally misunderstood, we need not waste time in trying to persuade him that his use of the word is not the right one. What we must be clear about is that a new use of the word is not a new statement of fact. We must be clear that what we are differing about is a verbal problem and not a factual one.

Unfortunately many such arguments are about general concepts which are so important to people that they think that they understand them intuitively, without ever having to define them. In these cases it is not always obvious when a new meaning is being proposed. I once attended a lecture at which a distinguished academic spoke on the subject of 'What is Freedom?' It seemed that what he meant by freedom was not being able to do exactly as you pleased, but living within a particular set of rules. During the questions afterwards it became apparent that many members of the audience regarded these rules as rather old-fashioned and repressive. In one sense, the lecturer spent an hour and a half explaining to us (in admirable detail) his new definition of the word 'freedom' and the questioners afterwards were saying why they thought that it was a bad definition. This suggests that the whole exercise was a complete waste of time.

However, there were real and important differences between the two sides. The lecturer was saying that even if you appear to have complete physical freedom, then your mind may impose its own restrictions. If, as he seemed to suggest, everyone who was given complete freedom of action went off and committed crimes, then in one sense, they would not be free because they were all doing the same thing. So the real difference was whether the kind of freedom that comes from having no physical limits imposed on your behaviour is a better thing or a worse thing than living the way he wanted us to. But he would probably not have got much of an audience if he had given a talk entitled 'Dr —'s Ideas About How You Ought To Behave'. On the other hand, if he had extended his argument to say that true freedom only comes when you are in prison, because there you are released from having to organize your own life, and your mind has complete freedom, it would have been far more obvious that what he was doing was presenting a new definition.

In this chapter we have been discussing those subjects of dispute that are factual and comparing them with those that are merely verbal. There is some danger of giving the impression that it is only the factual questions that are important and that questions of how to use words are not important. That certainly would be a wrong idea. We want to avoid mistaking verbal questions for factual ones but, when we have done that, we still have the problem of how to deal with verbal questions. We can only hope to settle a question of fact by using observations or research to discover what is really the case. Then we have to use words to convey the case to other people as clearly and unambiguously as we can. This is obviously important, but it is not always very easy. Later chapters will be concerned with these problems.

3

The meanings of words

A COMMON FORM of crooked thinking is to use the same word with different meanings in the course of an argument. This is often effective because it is difficult to detect in the heat of the moment. For this reason one should always beware when discussing words which have indefinite or changing meanings. Our old friends 'democracy' and 'freedom' are frequently used in this way because they have so many meanings.

If somebody told you that it is extremely dangerous to keep cats in the house, because some of them are notorious man-eaters, you would probably think that either he was mad, or he did not understand the difference between the word 'cat' applied to the small domestic pussy-cat and the word 'cat' meaning a member of the cat family, which includes lions and tigers.

However, arguments of this type are often overlooked. For instance, the writer of an article in *Time* magazine attacked the idea that you can prevent people taking 'revolutionary action' in Latin America by dealing with the so-called 'root causes' – poverty, misery and hunger. The writer's argument was that Arab terrorism, which he also called 'revolutionary action', was not directly motivated by poverty, misery and hunger in the Israeli-occupied West Bank, but rather by antagonism to Western influences and their effect on the Islamic way of life. His conclusions about 'root causes' may well have been correct, but what is more doubtful is whether 'revolutionary action' in Latin America is the same thing and has the same causes as the 'revolutionary action' taken by Palestinian terrorists (or freedom fighters, depending on your point of view). Revolutionary action in Latin America has usually been directed towards overthrowing the political system and government within a country, with the reform of land ownership being an important aim. The targets for this action are almost always within the revolutionaries' own country. The primary aim of Palestinian revolutionary action is not to achieve a social revolution, but to remove the Israelis and to create a Palestinian state, though the anti-Western motives the writer described may also exist. These revolutionary actions are often aimed at citizens of other countries which are not directly involved in the conflict.

The use of a single phrase 'revolutionary action' to describe different activities going on in widely separated parts of the globe implies that both have the same causes. But the difference between separate groups of people calling themselves 'revolutionaries' is clearly an important one, which will not go away by using the same word for both.

I saw a similar misuse of language in a pamphlet produced by the organization 'Aims for Freedom'. In it they gave a list of the ten basic freedoms that they wanted to preserve. Nine of the items in this list fitted into the usual idea of what we think of as freedom – not having other people deciding what you can and cannot do. The freedom not to pay taxes, to get your children educated where you want, and so on, fall within this definition of 'freedom'. However, the last essential freedom was 'the freedom to be defended against our country's enemies'. 'Freedom', as used here, means something quite different, since 'the freedom not to have to pay for the upkeep of an army' would be equally suited for inclusion in the list. In this case 'freedom' is being used in the woolly sense of 'something that we approve of' that I discussed in Chapter 2 and is not at all the same as 'freedom' in the other cases. (Incidentally, some extreme 'libertarians' in the USA do actually regard 'the freedom to be defended against our country's enemies' as a denial of freedom, and believe that people should be allowed to run their defence policy on a private enterprise basis. This

view at least has the benefit of consistency, even if the prospect of

The meanings of words

free-market forces determining which private army is to look after your security may be a little alarming.)

One of the situations in which there is most danger of our thought going wrong through changing meanings of words is when we are using such national names as Britain, America, Germany and Russia. Muddles in thought matter most when they have serious practical consequences, and few muddles have more serious consequences than the loose use of national names. Enthusiasm for war, international misunderstanding and failure to condemn cruelty can all result from failure to be clear as to when we are using national names with different meanings.

Let us imagine, for example, a speech that might be given by an American politician urging a hostile approach to Russia.

> We must resist Russia's aggression wherever it takes place. Throughout her history she has attempted to expand her empire and always followed a quest for power and domination, betraying her allies and launching unprovoked attacks on weaker countries. In the eighteenth and nineteenth centuries she pursued a policy of expansionism in Siberia and around the Black Sea, paying no attention to the interests and wishes of the inhabitants of those areas. In the First World War, she betrayed her Allies and made a separate peace with Germany, allowing the Germans to transfer vast armies to the Western Front to fight against her former Allies. Despite their contrasting political philosophies she made common cause with Hitler's Germany and left Britain to stand alone against the fascists for two years, meanwhile sharing the spoils of Poland's defeat and slaughtering the flower of her manhood in the Katyn massacre. When Hitler attacked Russia in turn she had the impertinence to demand support from the Allies she had betrayed two years earlier. She took advantage of the unwillingness of the Allies to fight further, to subjugate the defenceless small countries of central Europe behind the Iron Curtain. Even as Russian power waned, her ambition led her to attack Afghanistan and to support proxy wars in Africa and other parts of the world.

Even today she engages in cyber attacks against former satellite states that try to establish their independence from her. In view of this we remain suspicious of Russia and her ambitions. For our own safety, and for the sake of world peace, we never relax our vigilance against Russian aggression.

The word 'Russia', or the pronoun 'she' standing for it, occurs many times in this passage. The passage can only be a reasonable argument if the word 'Russia' is used to refer to the same thing every time that it occurs. But does it?

It is by no means clear what 'Russia' stands for in the first and second sentences. Certainly it does not, either here or anywhere else in the passage, just stand for the areas of ground that are now marked as 'Russia' on a map, for an area of ground cannot be a threat to peace or invade another piece of ground, or make or break a treaty. It may stand either for all or for some of the inhabitants of that area of ground or for the more abstract idea of that unity that makes a separate nation. The practical implications of the sentence do, of course, very considerably depend on which meaning 'Russia' is here meant to have.

The third sentence is easier. The first 'Russia' stands for Russian tsars and their advisers and senior officers in the eighteenth and nineteenth centuries, but the 'she' that comes next stands for something quite different. The alliance with the western Allies was made by the imperial government; by the time of the peace with the Germans the revolution had taken place and the new government did not feel bound by that agreement. In the sixth sentence the first 'she' refers to Joseph Stalin.

If the speaker had wanted to make his meaning perfectly clear he would have had to replace the word 'Russia' each time it occurred by some form of words which indicated exactly what he meant. Then his speech would run something like this.

We must resist Russia's aggression wherever it takes place. Throughout her history she has attempted to expand her empire and always followed a quest for power and domination, betraying her allies and launching unprovoked attacks on weaker countries. In the eighteenth and nineteenth centuries the Tsarist government pursued a policy of expansionism in Siberia and around the Black Sea, paying no attention to the interests and wishes of the inhabitants of those areas. In the First World War, the revolutionary government withdrew from the alliance that the Tsarist government had made with the Allies and made a separate peace with Germany, allowing the Germans to transfer vast armies to the Western Front to fight against her former Allies. Despite their contrasting political philosophies Joseph Stalin made common cause with Hitler's Germany and left Britain to stand alone against the fascists for two years, meanwhile sharing the spoils of Poland's defeat and slaughtering the flower of her manhood in the Katyn massacre. When Hitler attacked the USSR Stalin had the impertinence to demand support from the Allies he had betrayed two years earlier. Stalin took advantage of the unwillingness of the Allies to fight further, to subjugate the defenceless small countries of central Europe behind the Iron Curtain. Even as Soviet power waned, Stalin's successors attacked Afghanistan and supported proxy wars in Africa and other parts of the world. The post-communist government of the Russian Confedera-tion today engages in cyber attacks against former satellite states that try to establish their independence of her. In view of this it is not surprising that we remain suspicious of Russia and her ambitions. For our own safety, and for the sake of world peace, we never relax our vigilance against Russian aggression.

This speech still has defects from the point of view of straight thinking, but in its new form it has the merit of saying exactly what it means without confusion by shifting meanings. For that reason it has lost most of its value as propaganda. The conclusions of the argument may still be correct, but clearly some of the intermediate steps are missing. To what extent do the attitudes that make a country acquire a government which is likely to wage aggressive war persist from generation to generation?

The Russian ruling elite of the eighteenth and nineteenth centuries undoubtedly saw its role as one of military expansion. Stalin's reasons **33** for extending Soviet influence between the 1930s and 1950s were far more complicated, including paranoia, megalomania, a legitimate fear of encirclement and being overwhelmed by the Western democracies, and possibly even a genuine desire to export communism. The connection between Stalinist and post-Stalinist Soviet foreign policy and current-day Russian activities is even more complicated.

This may all seem like nit-picking but it is actually rather important. By using national names in a loose way, people construct arguments which hide many doubtful assumptions. I am not denying the existence of national characteristics. There were almost certainly features in Russian society which resulted in a policy of aggression towards other countries in Europe and Asia, just as there were features in British policy which led to a policy of aggression towards non-Europeans. However, using national characteristics in a comic-book way makes a nonsense out of trying to draw lessons from history. People do not use such simple ideas to understand the history of their own country; there is no reason why they should do so when describing what has happened in other countries.

Every time that we use phrases such as 'the greatness of Ruritania', 'Ruritania did so-and-so' or 'the interests of Ruritania', we should make sure that we know exactly what 'Ruritania' means in each case. In particular we should be sure when it stands for the whole group of inhabitants of Ruritania, and when it does not. If it is likely to refer to a small group of people ruling the country or exerting influence through their wealth, we should not feel ourselves too concerned in their interests, nor be too ready to sacrifice our lives for them.

It is in wartime that clear thinking on this topic is most important. When someone appeals to your patriotism it is likely that they want you to take a mental short-cut. While it may be worth fighting for certain qualities or values that one's country represents, it is not worth fighting for an ill-defined abstract concept such as 'my country, right or wrong'. There are good and bad things within every country, and it is best to make sure that you are fighting for the good things.

The habit of using words with two or more meanings without clearly distinguishing them can lead us into much faulty thinking. A much worse form of the same disease is that of using a word with no **34** clear meaning but only a general tendency in some direction. Then we are guilty of woolliness, which is a fault that makes accurate thought and reasonable discussion impossible.

In order to be woolly it is not necessary that a statement should also be difficult to comprehend. It often is, and more or less deliberate obscurity is often a cloak for woolliness. But the simplest statement may be woolly if it does not have a clear meaning to the person making it. This is particularly liable to happen with abstract words. Such words, for example, as 'principle', 'wealth' and 'spiritual' have meanings which can never be conveyed by a simple picture of an object or action, or of a relation between objects and actions. Their proper meaning is a kind of summary or abstraction of many different things.

We all hear many such words which at first carry no meaning for us at all, and we are quite likely to take them into our vocabulary before we know exactly what they mean. To obtain clear meanings for any but the common names of real objects requires a certain amount of mental effort, and idleness leads us to be content with taking many words into our speech and thought without making this effort. We should get rid of woolliness from our own minds before we consider how we can cope with that of other people. We can begin by looking up definitions. It is a useful rule to look up new words in the dictionary before starting to use them ourselves.

However, new words are only part of the problem. How often, when you use words like 'justice', 'equality', or 'intelligence', have you thought exactly what you mean by them? It is important when you start arguing, or reading an article which uses these kinds of words, that you are aware of what you and others think that they mean. If you do not, you will end up in the kind of situation described in Chapter 2.

While the use of dictionary definitions should prevent us from using words in a shifting or woolly way, we need more than that to use them effectively. Let us suppose, for example, that we have come across a technical term that is new to us. We wish to understand it when we read it, and also to be able to use it in our own talking and writing. We can look the word up in a dictionary or on the internet. If the real or virtual dictionary is a good one, we shall now have a clear and unambiguous account of how the word is used, either in general speech from the standard dictionary, or in scientific language **35** if we have consulted a technical dictionary. We shall discover from the dictionary how to describe the use of the new term and we shall know from the dictionary definition that a number of ways of using it that we previously have been tempted to adopt are wrong.

Knowing how to describe the use of a word is not, however, enough to ensure that we shall either understand its use or be able to use it in the proper way. The situation is rather as if we have read an accurate description of a deep-sea fish, but found this description insufficient to enable us to draw the fish or even to recognize it if we saw it.

In order to understand how a word should be used it is also important to have concrete examples of its use. The giving of illustrations is a useful device for keeping one's thinking in touch with reality. We should, in the course of reading, talking or thinking, challenge ourselves to give particular examples as illustrations of general statements. Otherwise the abstract terms we use may be so devoid of meaning to us that our thought has lost touch with reality.

We must not, of course, make the mistake of supposing that a single simple illustration exhausts the meaning of an abstract passage. Abstract terminology is a shorthand way of expressing a large collection of particular facts. Success in abstract thinking means that we can think of the whole group of facts as a class and not only of the particular members of it which we may have chosen for illustration. The challenge is to make use of abstract thinking to discuss complex issues in a practical manner while not forgetting that the words that we use are an imperfect description of that complexity.

4

Definition and some of its difficulties

I F WE WANT our thoughts to be clear, and to communicate them effectively to other people, we must be able to fix the meanings of the words we use. When we use a word where the meaning is not certain we may well be asked to define it. Many definitions follow a standard pattern. They state the general class or group to which the thing being defined belongs, and also the particular characteristic that distinguishes it from all the other members of the class. Thus we may define a whale as 'a marine mammal that spouts'. 'Marine mammal' in this definition describes the general class to which whales belong (though they do, of course, belong to other general classes such as marine animals with fins, legless animals and so on, which could be used in alternative definitions); and 'spouts' indicates the particular property that distinguishes whales from other marine animals such as fishes, seals, jellyfish and lobsters. In the same way, we can define 'democracy' as 'a system of government in which the people themselves rule', and 'brandy' as an alcoholic drink distilled from grapes.

There are, of course, other kinds of definitions. We may, for example, find it hard to think of a suitable definition for the word 'animal', so we say that an animal is a thing such as a rabbit, fish or dog. Similarly, we may say that a religion is a system such as Christianity, Islam, Judaism or Buddhism. This way of indicating the meaning of a term by listing examples of what it includes is of limited usefulness. If **37** we defined our use of the word 'animal' as above, our hearers might, for example, be doubtful whether a sea-anemone or a slug was to be included in the class of things called 'animals'. It is, however, a useful way of supplementing a definition if the definition itself is pre-cise without being easily understandable. If, for example, we explain what we mean by 'religion' by saying: 'A religion is a system of beliefs and practices connected with the spiritual world, such as Christianity, Islam, Judaism, Buddhism and so on', we may succeed in making our meaning clearer than it would be if we had given the definition alone.

Definitions can fail to serve their purpose if they give as the distin-guishing characteristics of the class something which either does not belong to all members of the class or does belong to things outside the class. Thinking, for example, of the most obvious difference between a rabbit and a cabbage, we might be tempted to define an animal as a living organism that is able to move about. This would combine both faults mentioned above, since some animals (e.g. some shellfish such as the oyster) are not able to move about for the whole or for part of their lives, while some plants (various single-celled algae) do swim about. Of course, anyone who used the above definition might claim to be defining 'animal' in a new and original way to include mobile single-celled algae and to exclude oysters, but he would have failed to produce a definition which stated the ordinary use of the word 'animal'. It is more likely that someone using this definition had sim-ply failed to think through all its implications.

Definition is relatively easy when things fall conveniently into classes; it becomes more difficult when one is dealing with things that do not. Then many pitfalls lie in the path of the careless thinker. There is an old law of logic called the 'Law of the Excluded Middle', which says that A is either B or not B. Thus a piece of paper is either white or not white. There is a sense in which this is obviously true, yet the kind of thinking that it leads to can be dangerous and misleading when applied to the real world.

Let us consider the case of white paper. The whiteness of paper depends on the amount of light that it reflects to our eyes. We should call the paper on which this book is printed 'white' because it reflects a good deal of light and absorbs very little. Yet it does not reflect all light. If we sprayed it silver it might reflect more, but it would still not reflect all the light falling on it. If we coated it very lightly with something that made it reflect less light, we might still call it white. As we increased the depth of the coating, however, we should soon reduce the brightness of the surface so much that we would have to call it light grey, afterwards dark grey, and finally black. The fact that we called it black, however, would not mean that the surface reflected no light. If we coated it with charcoal it would reflect still less light and would, therefore, be even blacker, but it would still reflect some of the light that fell on it.

It seems, then, that white, grey and black papers do not fall into naturally separable classes. The trouble lies in the fact that whiteness is something papers can have in any quantity; no paper is 100 per cent white and there is no real dividing line between paper that has enough whiteness to be called white and that which does not. We want, however, to use the words 'white', 'grey' and 'black' because they stand for real and important differences, and if we are to use them exactly we must adopt the device of definition for making their meanings clear.

For most practical purposes we do not have to be exact in our use of these terms, and it does not matter very much that one person will call a paper 'light grey' while another calls it 'dirty white', but there might be purposes for which it was necessary to leave no doubt of our use of these terms – for example if the paper is required for house decoration. Then we should have to make an arbitrary dividing line for our classification, defining a white paper, for example, as one that reflected at least 80 per cent of the light falling on it and a black paper as one that reflected not more than six per cent of the light falling on it, while a grey paper was defined as one that lay anywhere between these limits. Although what we have done in making these definitions is quite proper and may be useful, we have introduced a certain danger of crooked thinking, for we have used three words – 'white', 'grey' and 'black' – as if they stood for distinct classes, whereas there is continuous variation by imperceptible steps from the purest white to the darkest black. Such a way of thinking can cause confusion, since it may lead us to overlook the fact that we may have two white papers (reflecting, let us say, 81 per cent and 95 per cent) and a grey paper (reflecting 79 per cent) such that the difference between the grey and one of the whites is far less than the difference between the two **39** whites. In other words, it may lead us to think that there are sharper distinctions than there really are.

Any muddles in thought that result from ignoring this property of continuous variation in whiteness, greyness and blackness are, of course, unimportant. But similar muddles occur where they are important. 'Sane' and 'insane', 'good' and 'bad', and 'intelligent' and 'stupid' are pairs of opposites that show this property of continuous variation.

When we are using separate words to distinguish two extremes showing continuous variation between them, we are making a sharp distinction where there is actually none. We must constantly be aware of the continuity between sanity and insanity, between goodness and badness and between criminality and socially responsible behaviour. The difficulty is recognized in everyday speech as that of knowing 'where to draw the line'. Where no sharp dividing lines exist, the use of sharply different words to distinguish classes of facts which show continuous variation may distort the realities we are talking about.

The way in which the ignoring of continuous variation leads to crooked arguments may be illustrated as follows. In 2001 George Bush made the following statement following the September 11th attacks on the World Trade Towers in New York. 'Every nation in every region now has a decision to make. Either you are with us, or you are with the terrorists.' This is clearly not the case. Different countries may show different levels of support or opposition to the US 'War on Terror', and are not confined to these two opposed positions. All arguments that say: 'An X must be either Y or not-Y' must be treated as unsound if Y is a characteristic that shows continuous variation, and should be dealt with by pointing out that the sharp distinction between Y and not-Y implied by the speaker does not fit with the facts.

This is the first kind of crooked thinking into which we may be led when dealing with facts showing continuous variation; we may make sharp distinctions in speech where none exists in fact. There is another which is the opposite of this: we may deny the reality of differences because there is continuous variation between the different things. We can immediately see the error of claiming that there is no difference between white and black because we can pass from one to the other by a series of small steps, but an exactly parallel argument is often used to deny the reality of differences in matters that are of more practical importance.

A very old example illustrates the kind of error that is involved. It is possible to cast doubt on the reality of the difference between a bearded and a clean-shaven man by a process beginning with the question of whether a man with one hair on his chin has a beard. The answer is clearly 'No'. Then one may ask whether two hairs on a man's chin is a beard. Again, the answer must be 'No'. It is the same with three, four, etc. At no point can our opponent say 'Yes', for if he answered 'No' for, let us say, 29 hairs, and 'Yes' for 30, it is easy to ridicule the suggestion that the difference between 29 and 30 hairs is the difference between having and not having a beard. Yet by this process of adding one hair at a time we can reach a number of hairs that would undoubtedly make up a beard. The trouble is that the difference between a beard and no beard is like the difference between black and white, a difference between two extremes that have no sharp dividing line between them but a continuous gradation.

In this argument, the fact of continuous variation has been used to undermine the reality of the difference. Because there was no sharp dividing line, it has been suggested that there is no difference. This is clearly a piece of crooked argument that would be easy to detect, so long as it was used about beards and not about anything which engaged our emotions more strongly.

A similar error lay at the back of the mind of the man who loaded his camel one straw at a time, hoping that the additional weight of a single straw would never be enough to injure the camel's back. When at length the camel's back broke, he attributed it to the extra weight of the last straw. He supposed that because there was no sharp line between a moderate load and a severe overload, there was therefore no difference between them. Again this is a mistake that no reasonable person would make.

We do, however, sometimes hear people arguing that there is no difference between a criminal and a supposedly law-abiding citizen, because there is no one who has not broken the law in a minor way, usually by some kind of motoring offence. People proposing this argument may also say that the reason why these apparently law-abiding citizens have never been caught in a major criminal act is because **41** they have not had the opportunity, or the need, to perpetrate a major crime. The truth is, of course, that the difference between those people who are habitual criminals and those who are not is a major difference in society. The importance of this difference is not affected by the fact that there is no sharp dividing line between criminals and other people, nor by the fact that some apparently sober citizens are secret criminals. The justification for using a word like 'criminal' is the same as the justification for using the word 'white', and the use of the word is open to precisely the same dangers of creating sharply distinct classes where none exists in fact. This danger, however, is not to be dealt with by denying the reality of the difference.

It is sometimes argued that breaking the speed limit is not important because the difference in speed between driving just below the legal limit and driving just above it is infinitesimally small. The police do not usually stop people who are driving slightly faster than the speed limit so it is suggested that the limit should be raised. Presumably once this was done people would drive just a little bit faster still. This process could be continued with each new speed limit until the speed people drove at was limited by the power of their cars rather than the legal limit. Just because speed shows continuous variation does not mean that one should not define a limit above which one is driving too fast.

The argument of the beard is also sometimes used against the important distinction between neutral and emotionally charged words discussed in the first chapter of this book. It has been suggested that this distinction cannot be a real one because the words that we use may be more or less emotionally charged so that we can draw no fine line between those that are neutral and those that do have some emotional overtone. This, of course, is the case, but this is not inconsistent with there being a real and important difference between an almost completely neutral term such as 'not easily influenced' and the highly charged term 'pig-headed'. The theory of evolution says that humankind has evolved in small stages from single-celled organisms, but this does not mean that we should deny the difference between ourselves and amoebae, or even other apes.

Even when we are considering classes of things that show an indefinite series of steps in passing to their opposites, it is still necessary to

use words with exact indications of their meanings. We may also use definitions as a way of showing what we mean, while being aware that in these cases definitions may involve arbitrary dividing lines which may differ from those used by other people (such as the 80 per cent reflection of light in our definition of 'white'). Yet the practice of defining one's terms may have dangers, since it tends to create ideas that are too precise to fit the facts that they are intended to describe. This may be no help to clear thinking if it still results in creating clear distinctions in our minds which do not exist in reality. The device of badgering one's opponent to define his terms may sometimes be a piece of crooked argument, since it may be an invitation to him to provide clear-cut ideas which have little relation to the complexity of the facts under discussion. The world is a complicated place and we should always remain aware of its complexity.

5

Good and bad definitions

THE LAST CHAPTER was about what makes a definition and the problems that inevitably come from having to define the words that we use. This chapter is concerned with how some definitions may be good and others bad, even if they are properly constructed.

As I have already mentioned, there is no fundamental reason why you should not use any word in any way that you please. There is no law of nature stating that the word 'aubergine' should be used to describe a kind of vegetable rather than, say, an article of clothing (and over the course of time it is not impossible for such a change in usage to occur). However, there is a serious risk of confusion if you use a word in a new way. This is particularly true if you do not specifically define the word in the course of a conversation, speech, argument or piece of writing. In practice, one very rarely does so, so the definitions of words that one uses tend to be implicit, rather than explicit. By 'implicit', I mean that the definition is not actually stated, but only becomes apparent by the way that you use the word. Whereas an unconventional explicit definition is likely to appear obviously ridiculous, an unusual implicit definition may be used as a dishonest form of argumentation. Perhaps instead of saying that some definitions are unusual, it would be better to say that some definitions are good, and some are bad. If we use a bad implicit definition then we are, intentionally or not, using a dishonest argument.

For instance, an extreme left-wing speaker might give a speech in which he referred to people who voted for the Conservative party as 'fascists'. If he made it clear at the beginning that when he said 'fascists' he was simply referring to Conservative voters, he would be guilty of using a word in an unusual way and of being unnecessarily offensive. If, however, he used the word 'fascist' in this way without saying what he was doing, he would also be guilty of seriously misleading his listeners.

So how can we decide if a definition, implied or explicit, is a good one or not? A good definition, and thus a good way of using a word, should fit the following rules.

1 It should conform to normal usage as far as possible. Everything that people usually describe using a particular word should fit into its definition.
2 The meaning of the word should be distinct from those of other words. There is no point in using a word in such a broad way that its meaning does not differ from that of a range of other words.
3 The same name should be given to things that are basically similar. Another way of putting this is to say that the structure of language should correspond with the structure of the world of fact that we wish to describe. For instance, a category that placed sharks and whales together would be less satisfactory than one that combined dolphins and whales.
4 It should not be used in such a way as to conceal an inbuilt emotional attitude.

I have already discussed the problems arising from using words with implied emotional content. The other side of the coin involves redefining otherwise neutral words in such a way as to indicate your attitude towards the thing defined. The purpose of a definition should be to clarify how you are going to use words, not to indicate your attitude towards the thing defined.

A typical muddle that results from not making this distinction is the one produced by people who think that they prove their breadth of mind by using a very broad definition of 'religion', such as the one in *Merriam-Webster's Online Dictionary* which is 'a cause, principle, or system of beliefs held to with ardour and faith.' This contrasts with the more restrictive definition in the *The Concise Oxford Dictionary* (1990), which is 'human recognition of superhuman controlling power and especially of a personal God entitled to obedience.' This would exclude some Buddhist sects, some Christians who do not believe in an all-powerful controlling God and any believers in more than one god.

In reality there is no moral value attached to a wide or a narrow use of a word; neither tolerance nor charity towards those who differ from us in religion depends on our use of the word. It is purely a question of practical convenience. A narrow use of the word 'religion' has two inconveniences. First, it uses the word 'religion' for something that already has its own name (in this case 'monotheism'); there is obviously no point in having two different words to describe the same thing. Secondly, and more seriously, it leaves us without a word to describe other forms of belief such as ancestor worship or voodoo. If we are not to use the word 'religion' for these, we must find some other word for them. So all somebody using a narrow definition of 'religion' has done is to take a word that was serving a useful purpose and put it where it is useless. Someone using a restrictive definition is trying to say that he thinks that there is something better or more true about this kind of religion.

There are also objections from the viewpoint of convenience to defining 'religion' as 'a cause ... held with ardour and faith.' The definition is so vague that it does not fulfil the primary purpose of a definition, of making clear to what it is meant to be applied. Many football fans support their teams with ardour and faith. It does not seem likely that such beliefs are meant to be included in the word 'religion' when this is defined in such a way, but this definition might be taken to include them. There is also the same objection to this definition as was made to the very restricted definition: that if we are to use the word 'religion' in this way, we are left without a name for the class of things that includes Christianity, Buddhism, Islam, etc. But we do want a name for this class if we are ever to think or talk about it.

Definition is a process intended to make our thought clear and our
speech understandable to others. The use of definition as a means of

indicating opinions or valuation defeats its proper aim. Governments are no more immune than individuals to this fatuous use of language. In 1986 the US Government announced that it reserved the right to use for military purposes a space station which was to be jointly paid for by America and her European allies. It was thought that there might be a hostile response from the allies who had believed that the station was only to be used for 'peaceful' purposes. An Air Force official said that other countries might have misinterpreted a policy of restricting space ventures to 'peaceful purposes' as meaning non-military. 'We will limit our use of outer space for peaceful purposes,' he said. 'Our philosophy is that anything the United States does, including the Department of Defence, is in the name of peace . . .' I hardly need to point out that any other government in the world could make the same claim, but that would not make them any less likely to become involved in armed conflict.

The rules I have listed for making a good definition may on occasion conflict with each other. Since different people use words in slightly different ways, a definition that includes all the normal uses will be so broad that it fails to be distinct from other words. For instance, in Denmark, which is a very flat country, the fourth highest 'mountain' in the country is Himmelbjerget, which means 'the mountain reaching heaven' but is only 147 m above sea level. Someone from Nepal, who was used to very high mountains, would probably say that this was an extremely small hill. If our definition of 'mountain' included everything that both Danes and Nepalis call mountains, then it would be such a broad definition that it would be useless. It is fortunate that, for most of the time, it is not necessary to worry about the precise definition of 'mountain' (or indeed of most other words describing qualities that show continuous variation). There are likely to be very few situations in which substituting 'large hill' for 'small mountain' will result in confusion. When that is the case, we shall have to use a precise definition that may prove unattractive to either Danes or Nepalis, but that is impossible to avoid if we want the definition to be useful.

The second criterion for good use of language is using the same word for things that are really similar. Putting similar things together is the process of classification, which I mentioned briefly in Chapter 2. **47**

This is an essential feature of language, which allows us to cope with the enormous variety of objects and concepts in the world.

In theory there is no reason why we should not classify any objects in the same category. We might, for instance, put razors, kangaroos and the small clouds that look like cotton wool together in one class, and call them 'gruds'. However, we should soon find that the concept of a grud was not very useful and we should not use the word much, because the objects in the category had very little in common. A useful category must clearly include things that do have something in common. However, some shared characteristics are more valuable than others. A category composed of flags, flans, flamingos and flannels includes words which share the first three letters, but this classification still has little point because there are few occasions when we feel a need to use 'fla-' words as a single category. Even putting together fire engines, blood and the Russian flag, because they are all red, is not useful, because colour is not the most important attribute of an object. Deciding what is may be a difficult task.

The most useful classification systems are those that show the characteristic of hierarchy. A *hierarchy* is a graded system of classification. Among the most familiar and obvious hierarchies are those of military units. Each soldier belongs to a section, which forms part of a platoon, which forms part of a company, which is part of a battalion, and so on right up to the highest levels of organization. An individual soldier can be classified by which section he belongs to, and also by which platoon, company, battalion, etc. he is a member of. A similar principle applies to classification of the natural world. For instance, a mallard duck is a member of the family that includes ducks and geese, which is part of the class of birds, which in turn falls within the group of vertebrates and then within the animal kingdom.

Hierarchies are the most efficient form of classification. This becomes obvious when we think of the way that the Post Office uses addresses. In theory everyone could just have their name, and that of their house, as an address. If the Post Office wanted to deliver a letter, they would have to look at a map to find out where to take it. This would be an incredible task. Even if one could get a map with everyone's name and house on it, it would be like hunting for a needle **48** in a haystack. Instead we have a hierarchical system of addresses.

The highest level of organization is the country; within this is the county or state, and at the next level down comes the city, town or village. At the lowest level is the street name and number. A very small country composed of ten counties, with ten cities in each, the cities having ten streets apiece, each with ten houses, would have a total of ten thousand addresses. Yet by using a hierarchical classification, we could describe the location of each house with a total of 40 different names and numbers.

Much the same applies to words. We do not have enough words to describe everything uniquely with a single word, so we must make sure that we use efficiently the ones we have got. Everything else being equal, the best definition is a simple one which fits into a hierarchy. The form of definition described in Chapter 4 – the general category in which something fits, together with its distinguishing features – is of this type. If a definition is complex, with lots of provisions and exceptions, it is unlikely to fit neatly into a hierarchical classification. It should, if at all possible, be avoided in the interests of economy.

One practical example that illustrates some of these difficulties is that of terrorism. If you were asked to define 'terrorism' you might say that it was 'an act of violence aimed at civilian morale rather than at military targets.' This is concise, and seems to contain the essence of what we mean by 'terrorism'. However, the definition covers some rather surprising types of violent action. For instance, according to this definition, the Allied bombing of German cities and the bombing of Hiroshima and Nagasaki were undoubtedly acts of terrorism, since their purpose was to bring an end to the war by undermining civilian resistance. On the other hand, the Taliban's roadside bombs aimed at killing British and American soldiers might not be counted as terrorism, if one believed that there was a chance of a purely military victory for the Taliban.

In fact, if we were to produce a definition which included everything that is normally described in the newspapers and by politicians as 'terrorism', and excluded such actions as blanket bombing of cities, then we might come up with something along these lines: 'acts of violence by small groups of people, who are not wearing uniforms, directed against citizens of countries that are not at war with their **49** own country.' This definition is unsatisfactory. It is much more complicated than the one suggested before and does not point to a single idea that one might call the essence of terrorism.

In this case it does not seem possible to produce a definition that satisfies all the rules I suggested at the beginning of the chapter. Either one can use a definition that fits with normal usage or else one that better reflects the reality of the thing being defined. In this case it is essential that the general idea of terrorism should not be discussed without it being explicitly defined. In discussion of similarly controversial topics where bad implicit definitions are commonly used, we should also make it clear exactly what definition we are using.

6

All and some

STRANGE AS IT seems today, there used to be many areas in Scotland where it was impossible to buy an alcoholic drink. For instance, in Stewarton in Ayrshire, all pubs were closed between 1920 and 1967. This is because it was widely believed that most social ills were the result of excessive drinking and in those days many people believed that prohibition was the solution. In 1922 Winston Churchill even lost his parliamentary seat in Dundee to a prohibitionist candidate, Ernest 'Neddy' Scrymgeour. An act of parliament – the Temperance Act of Scotland – was passed in 1913 allowing districts and parishes to vote to ban the sale of alcoholic drinks. This provision remained in force until 1976 and over a thousand local votes on prohibition were held – mostly between 1920 and 1930. In many places opponents of prohibition sought to have further polls to allow the pubs to re-open.

At that time, I passed through an area in which there was to be such a poll. There I saw the following poster: IF LIBERTY IS LOST, SLAVERY REIGNS: VOTE REPEAL. The first part of this poster is an argument. As often happens in practice, a great part of the argument is left out, but we can easily supply the missing part, and the result is an argument which, at first sight, looks correct. It would run like this: (1) A condition in which liberty is lost is one in which slavery reigns. (2) Prohibition is a condition in which liberty is lost. (3) Therefore, prohibition is a condition in which slavery reigns.

This has the general form of a correct argument since, in skeleton form, it says: A is B; B is C; therefore A is C. The statements (1) and (2) are both correct, so the conclusion must also be correct provided that 51 words used in both (1) and (2) have the same meaning each time they are used. However, as we shall see, this important provision is not fulfilled, so the conclusion is not proved. Moreover, the conclusion is wrong in fact. Inability to buy a glass of beer may be a bad thing but it is not slavery.

The fallacy lies in the omission of the word 'all' or 'some' in front of 'liberty'. Statement (1) is true only if 'all' is inserted, while (2) is true only if 'some' is inserted. The fallacy is quite clear in the extended form of the argument, but is concealed in its original shortened form, 'If liberty is lost, slavery reigns.' It is true that under prohibition some liberty is lost – the liberty to buy alcoholic drink. But the argument suggests, quite falsely, that under prohibition all liberty is lost, for it is only when all liberty is lost that slavery can be said to reign.

This can be put in a more general way by saying that a common form of dishonest argument is the statement 'A is B' when 'some A is B' would be true; but 'all A is B' is what the hearer is meant to accept. The world of propaganda and of argumentation is full of such statements.

The extermination of Jews in Nazi Germany, of aristocrats in the French Revolution and the persecution of minority groups in various countries in our own times are all examples of the readiness of people to act on the statement that 'all Xs are evil' when X stands for those of another nation, race or creed. Yet it is apparent to an impartial observer that the truth is merely that 'some Xs are evil' (as are some not-Xs). Cruelty and injustice are resulting now, as they have throughout the history of the world, from this piece of crooked thinking.

It is not, of course, the case that all general statements of the form 'all Xs are Y' must necessarily be untrue. That would be absurd. I am only concerned to point out that they very often are untrue and that we may be led to overlook this if the word 'all' is left out. Then they escape challenge because it looks as if they meant 'some Xs are Y' although they are used in argument as if 'all Xs are Y' were true.

One reason why we are inclined to say or to imply 'all' in a sentence which would be true with the word 'some' is that a sentence with 'some' says so little. Suppose that we say quite truthfully: 'Some red-haired people are excitable.' We have said so little that it was hardly worth saying at all, for there are some excitable people who do not have red **52** hair, and some people with red hair are certainly not excitable.

Clearly we need a way of saying something about the connection between excitability and redness of hair which means more than the simple statement with 'some', and yet is not the same as the obviously untrue statement with 'all'. This statement, when we have it, may, of course, be true or false. The first step is to consider exactly what we want to say; then we can find out whether or not it is true. There is, in fact, such a form of statement. It is found even in everyday speech as the statement: 'I think that red-haired people are more inclined to be excitable than other people.' Or, of course, one may think that they are less inclined to be excitable than other people. A man who has taught himself to think in such terms is less likely to fall into the type of error we have been discussing. Also he is more likely to appreciate that it is difficult to get sufficient evidence to prove such a statement, and that one cannot get very good evidence from everyday observations.

Social sciences such as psychology, economics and sociology are much concerned with relationships of this kind. Human beings are too variable for it to be likely that, in the sciences dealing with them, one will find many true statements in the form 'all Xs are Y'. Much more commonly the form of statement that has to be used is of the kind: 'There is a tendency for Xs to be Y.' If we say that there is a tendency for red-haired people to be excitable, we do not mean that all red-haired people are excitable, and we do not imply that all people without red hair are calm. We do not even mean to imply that there are more excitable people with red hair than there are excitable people who are not red-haired. What is meant is that there is a larger proportion of excitable people among the red-haired than among the people whose hair is not red. In other words, anybody who has red hair is more likely to be an excitable person than someone who does not have red hair.

We now have a reasonable form of statement to inquire about. It still may not be true. If we wanted to discover whether it is true or not we should have to conduct an investigation such as the following. Let us suppose that we studied a random sample of 1000 people – a large enough group to be taken as a fair sample of the population as a whole. Let us suppose that we divided those into groups of 200 who had red hair and 800 who did not. We would have to define what we **53** mean by 'excitable' and 'calm', and devise a means of testing which group each fits into. Then let us suppose that we divided each of these groups into those who were and those who were not excitable, and found 50 excitable people among the red-haired and 100 among the not red-haired. We have now divided our 1000 people into four classes, and every one of the 1000 must fall into one or other of these classes. The result is summarized in this diagram.

50 excitable red-haired	150 calm red-haired
100 excitable not red-haired	700 calm not red-haired

Now these figures contain a complete answer to our question: Do red-haired people tend to be excitable? Let us examine them carefully and see what they mean. There are only half as many excitable people with red hair as there are without. But this does not mean that red-haired people are less likely to be excitable than others because there is a smaller total number with red hair. In fact, one-quarter of the red-haired are excitable and only one-eighth of the others. So the answer to the question indicated by these figures is 'yes'. A bookmaker could safely give you odds of about seven to one against a particular person without red hair being excitable; but he could only offer you about three to one against a particular red-haired person being excitable. The chance of a red-haired person being excitable will be just double the chance of a person without red hair being excitable.

The figures given above are not, of course, genuine ones. They were invented by me as an illustration of what was meant by a tendency for Xs to be Y. So far as I know, the necessary statistical research into the association between red hair and excitability has never been done; if it were, I do not suppose that it would show any tendency whatever for red-haired people to be more excitable than anyone else.

The method of analysis given above is one that will be familiar to those who have studied statistics. I have given only the elementary part of the argument and omitted complications which would have to be considered by a research worker before deciding whether there was a real relationship between the two characteristics being investigated, or whether the results might be 'chance' effects: that is, an

accidental property of the sample being studied. Instructions on how to discover this are to be found in any statistical textbook. In fact, with a sample as large as 1000 and a disproportion as great as 50:150 and 100:700 the researcher would be entirely justified in drawing the conclusion that there was a tendency for the two characteristics of red hair and excitability to go together.

If we realize that this is the kind of evidence that would be required to justify the conclusion that red-haired people tend to be excitable, we can see how absurd it would be if two men set themselves to argue on the question of whether red-haired men were excitable, and one of them said that they were, and 'proved' it merely by pointing to members of the red-haired, excitable class and of the non-red-haired, non-excitable class; while his opponent similarly 'proved' his case by pointing to the members of the non-excitable, red-haired class and the excitable, non-red-haired class. It would be about as easy for the second man as for the first, because in our group of 1000 he would have 100 of the one class and 150 of the other. Yet it is completely clear that neither of these two men would be proving his case at all. Furthermore it could not be proved in this way – a kind of argument we may call 'proof by selected instances'.

This is a trivial example, but the principles involved apply to more important questions. Suppose, for example, that the figures were those of the numbers of cigarette smokers and non-smokers who died of lung cancer. If in a properly selected sample, it were found that, of 200 cigarette smokers, ten died of lung cancer whereas among 800 non-smokers, four died of the disease, this would be sufficient proof that smokers were more likely to die of lung cancer. This distribution of figures would not itself be enough to prove that cigarette smoking caused lung cancer, since there are two other ways in which it could be explained. It might be that the fact of suffering from lung cancer caused the sufferers to smoke cigarettes. It might also be the result of the fact that certain people differed from others in some respect that made them more likely to smoke cigarettes and also more likely to die of lung cancer. The first of these alternative explanations has generally been regarded as too improbable for serious consideration, and the second is the one put forward by those who do not accept the explanation that cigarette smoking is a cause of lung cancer. The figures obtained on this problem do, in fact, make **55** it clear that there is a real association between cigarette smoking and the development of lung cancer, since roughly one in 20 smokers dies of lung cancer but only one in 200 non-smokers dies of the disease.

These figures do not in themselves prove that cigarette smoking causes lung cancer, although they suggest this as a possible explanation; there are other findings which indicate that it is also the right explanation. It is important to remember that a link between two things (a *correlation* in statistical language) does not necessarily mean that one causes the other. Thus if people who were likely to suffer from lung cancer were also more likely to take up smoking, there might be a tendency for lung cancer victims to be smokers, without the cancer being caused by smoking. Similarly an increase in concentrations of atmospheric carbon dioxide at the same time as global temperatures have increased, does not necessarily mean that one causes the other. Other types of evidence are necessary in order to demonstrate causal relationships.

There are many other disputed questions to which the same issues of 'all or some' apply. During wartime we are inclined to think of the enemy people as bad. Indeed, their supposed badness is often one of the reasons for fighting a war to the end and for making harsh peace terms when it is over. Yet before or after the war we do not think that all the people of the enemy nation are bad since often we will have known some of them personally and found them good and kindly people. We may, however, remain convinced that there is a strong tendency for the enemy people to be bad. Clearly the measurements necessary to establish this tendency have not been made, and there is no sufficient rational ground for asserting it rather than the contrary proposition that as large a proportion of good and kindly people are to be found among the enemy nationals as anywhere else.

This is clearly a question where we do not have the numerical evidence that would alone constitute sound proof, even if we could agree on some criterion for measuring goodness. There are other questions on which the required numerical proof is available, but which are nevertheless argued by the crude and inaccurate method of selected instance. We may take as an example the problem of whether capital

punishment is an effective deterrent of murder. Upholders of capital punishment can point to countries that have no capital punishment and a large number of murders, and those that have capital punishment and a small number of murders. Their opponents can point to countries with no capital punishment and few murders and to others with capital punishment and many murders. This is merely proof by selected instances and carries us no further.

The real proof is an examination of the numerical relationships of all these four classes such as we made earlier for the problem of excitability and red hair, and this examination does not appear to indicate any association between the frequency of murder in a country and the capital punishment of murderers in that country. However, this does not mean that there is no such association. In this case, there are few countries in some of the categories, and, as with the smoking example, there may be factors affecting both the incidence of murders and of capital punishment. What is true, however, is that the data on the relationship between capital punishment and murders in different countries is not evidence in the favour of the proposition that capital punishment is an effective deterrent of murder. This proposition may still be true or false.

There is a wide range of controversial statements on which discussion can be interminable because the form of the statement does not indicate whether 'all' or 'some' is meant. Examples of such statements are: 'Scotsmen are misers'; 'Black people are less intelligent than whites'; 'Women are less logical than men'; 'Bald men are sexy'; 'Accountants are boring'. All of these statements are meaningless as they stand, and cannot sensibly be either asserted or denied. They are meaningless because the subject is indeterminate. There is not one accountant but many. Some of these lead very exciting lives, most of them are neither particularly boring nor particularly exciting, some are excruciatingly dull. In the same way, some black men are intellectually brilliant while some white men are not. Some women are illogical but so are some men.

No doubt all these statements are made by people who really mean something else, and although they are nonsense in the form in which they are stated, they could be replaced by other statements that make sense and which a quantitative investigation might prove to be true or false. What then is at the back of the minds of those who **57** say: 'Black men are less intelligent than white men'? If we replace it by the statement: 'Every black man is less intelligent than every white man', we have said something that makes sense but which is manifestly false.

If we want a form of statement which is meaningful and which might be true or false, we must use some such form of words as that already discussed: 'There is a tendency for black men to be less intelligent than white men.' This statement is meaningful but it may not be true; whether it is or not can only be settled by measurement by suitable intelligence tests of a large random sample of black people and comparison with similar measurements for a comparable sample of white people.

This has been done. During the Second World War all men called up for the draft in the USA were subjected to IQ tests. The results showed that although the differences were slight, black people had lower average test scores than people of European descent (and they also showed that Japanese people and Jewish people had higher average scores than those of Anglo-Saxon descent).

There are obvious objections to these tests. First of all, IQ tests do not just measure 'native intelligence' but also the extent to which it has been developed. This is clearly strongly affected by environment. Someone who has grown up under conditions of poor nutrition, with relatively little intellectual stimulation, access to books, or leisure will be intellectually stunted. At the time these tests were carried out, black people in the USA had a considerably lower average standard of living than white people, and it is most probable that these differences in test score were largely determined by relative economic conditions and not by race. Indeed, it was found that the average IQ scores of black men from the Northern states were higher than those of white men from the economically less developed Southern states.

Since then a great deal of effort has been devoted to establishing whether there are inherited and racial differences in intelligence (or rather, average scores in IQ tests). People have tried to devise IQ tests that eliminate the influence of environment and they have tried to make comparisons between people with broadly similar environments. The results are hotly contested. What is certain is that any differences are minor; what is disputed is whether there are any differences at all.

The heat of this debate can be attributed to a confusion between 'all' and 'some'. Opponents of the idea of racial differences in IQ have the best of intentions, and are motivated by fear of what the revelation of racial differences in IQ might do to education policies. However, the concern over the scientific results is unjustified. What can be said is that there will almost certainly be some overall differences between the races in the scores obtained from any conceivable IQ test, regardless of how carefully they are controlled for the effects of environment. These differences may be rather small but will appear if a sufficiently large sample is tested, just as differences in IQ between people of different heights will probably be shown.

The more important question is whether these small differences, whichever way they go, should have any effect on our policy or behaviour. The short answer is 'no'. Let us imagine a class of 40 children, 20 of whom have blue hair and 20 of whom have green hair. If there was a ten per cent average difference in IQ – a much higher figure than anyone could expect for differences between the races in reality – then on average there would be 13 green-haired and seven blue-haired children in the top half of the class. It is clear that if we wanted to know how intelligent a child was, we could not do so reliably by looking at the colour of his or her hair. It would be ridiculous to suggest that standards were being dragged down so far by the blue-haired children that one would want to educate children separately on the basis of hair colour.

As long as the opponents of this kind of research act as if the result 'There is a small tendency for members of one race to have a higher IQ than those of another' is the same as 'All members of one race have a higher IQ than those of another', then this issue will attract much more attention than it deserves. It is not a very interesting piece of science, but that does not mean that one should attempt to deny or prevent the publication of its results. What is important is that one should understand the importance, or lack of importance, of any results that come out.

There are other problems of the same kind on which the answer is not known because no one has yet overcome the difficulties of getting the information necessary for their solution. 'Does imprisonment effectively deter people from committing crimes?'; 'Do less **59** academically able children perform better in mixed ability classes?'; and so forth. These are questions that could be answered by research, but conclusive answers have not yet been provided. It does not follow, however, that on such questions we must have no opinions. On practical questions of urgent importance we must make up our minds one way or the other, even when we know that the evidence is incomplete. To refuse to make up our minds is equivalent to deciding to leave things as they are (which is just as likely to be the wrong solution).

But the fact that we must make up our minds in practice is no reason for failing to think straight on such questions by mistaking incomplete for complete evidence. We must not suppose that our case can be proved by merely selecting instances favourable to our view, while we ignore other instances. If, for example, we are arguing in favour of imprisonment, it is not enough merely to give selected instances of people who have reformed after going to prison, and people who have reoffended after being given non-custodial sentences. Nor must we think that our case is disproved if our opponents similarly select instances of criminals who have reformed without going to prison and prisoners who have re-offended. Always we must be on the lookout for real evidence from an impartial study of the numerical relations of all four combinations of success and failure with imprisonment and non-custodial sentences, with all the possible confounding effects being taken into account. We must also remember that, in all such cases, real evidence can only come from extensive research and not by any casual thinking or argumentation we can do for ourselves.

Evidence-based research in the social sciences is much more difficult than in the physical sciences. It is usually not possible to set up a good experimental design, with two equivalent sets of subjects given different treatments, and then measurements taken to find out which works better. If we wanted to know whether capital punishment was an effective deterrent of crime, ideally we would randomly split the nations of the world into two and apply capital punishment to one half, and not to the other. After a few years, we should have a pretty good answer. However, in the real world such
60 experiments are seldom possible and social scientists have to rely on

'natural experiments', which are not so well controlled. As a result any analysis of data will be subject to multiple interpretations.

In the meantime, we have to make up our minds on such evidence as is available and that, we know, is incomplete. This means that although we must make up our minds definitely we must not do so finally, but we must be willing to be guided by experience, being sure that experience will lead us to change our minds on subjects about which we have felt most certain.

7

Some dishonest tricks in argument

WE HAVE ALREADY noticed that a statement of the form 'all Xs are Y' is very rarely true and is easily disproved. It is easily disproved for the obvious reason that a single instance of an X that is not Y is sufficient to overthrow it. If, for example, someone maintains that all pacifists are cowards, their opponent need point to only one pacifist who has shown courage by facing death bravely, and the case is overthrown. If, on the other hand, the more moderate proposition that *some* pacifists are cowards had been maintained, it could not have been defeated, for undoubtedly one or more examples of pacifists who were cowards could have been brought forward, and the contention would then be established.

This suggests that someone who maintains an extreme view (such as 'all Xs are Y') is very unlikely to win an argument. Many people consciously or unconsciously use a trick based on this principle, by driving their opponents to adopt a more extreme position than is necessary for their purpose. Against an incautious opponent, this can often be done simply by contradicting his moderate assertions until in the heat of the moment he puts forward more and more extreme views.

Let us suppose, for example, that two men are arguing about the condition of some country under a communist government such as Cuba. M maintains that the people are starving, that industry is hopelessly inefficient, and that the people are only kept from a successful uprising by terror. N holds against him the more moderate position that things are not as bad as M paints them, and that in some respects the workers are better off than they are in some non-communist countries. Clearly M is holding a position less easy to defend than the other, and we should expect N to win the argument. So he probably would if he were content to stick to the very moderate set of propositions that he has laid down, which are really all that is needed to make his point. As the argument goes on, however, M makes exaggerated statements of the bad conditions of workers in Cuba and, by a natural reaction, N makes equally wild statements of their prosperity, until he is maintaining a picture of universal well-being which his facts are quite insufficient to support. M now assumes the offensive and brings forward facts sufficient to overthrow the over-favourable view of the conditions in Cuba which N has been incautious enough to defend, and N loses the argument. Yet he had a winning case to begin with.

A person cautious in argument will not, however, be so easily led to court defeat. He will constantly reaffirm the moderate and defensible position with which he started, and the extreme statements of his opponent will be rebutted by evidence instead of leading on to equally extreme statements on the other side. Against such a person, however, a similar trick is used very commonly in a more blatantly dishonest way. He has asserted moderately and truly that 'some Xs are Y', but his opponent argues against the proposition that 'all Xs are Y'. If he answers his opponent's arguments at all, he can only do so by defending the proposition 'all Xs are Y'. Then he has fallen into the trap. If he avoids this by reasserting his original position, his opponent often brings against him a piece of nonsense which runs: 'But you ought logically to say that all Xs are Y if you think some Xs are Y.'

Let us call this the 'extension' of one's opponent's statement. It can be used by luring him on to extend it himself in the heat of controversy or, more impudently, by misrepresenting what he has said, or by the device of saying that 'he ought logically' to be defending the extended proposition. It is a device often used in argument, sometimes no doubt involuntarily; the remedy is always to refuse to accept an extension, but to reaffirm the position one really wants to defend. **63**

An example of an attempt to force an extension on to a speaker comes from a time of economic hardship in Great Britain. The speaker argued that, with so much distress amongst the less well off, the country could not afford heavy expenditure on costly luxuries, giving as an example opera performances subsidized by the state. This was a moderate and reasonable proposition. One of his hearers accused him afterwards of inconsistency in attacking all expenditure on what were considered non-essentials, since, presumably, the speaker had recreations of his own on which he spent money.

The speaker refused to have his proposition extended and reasserted his original statement that not all spending on recreation was undesirable, pointing out that he had already shown that this was his view by arguing that some spending on luxuries of this kind was desirable for everybody. His opponent now said: 'To be logically consistent, you ought to disapprove of all spending on luxuries if you disapprove of expenditure on opera.' To this unreasonable assertion I know of no satisfactory reply except to deny that there is any such logical necessity. The statement that 'Some spending on luxuries is socially desirable' is in no way incompatible with the statement that 'Some forms of spending on luxuries are socially undesirable.' It would, of course, be reasonable and proper to ask the speaker by what criteria he distinguished between the kind of spending on luxuries that was socially undesirable and the kind of luxury expenditure that he considered to be desirable or at least harmless. One might also consider whether the reasons he gave for objecting to subsidizing opera would also be reasons for condemning the speaker's own recreations. It is, however, not reasonable to misrepresent the speaker's contention that subsidizing opera was socially undesirable at that time by suggesting that he was condemning all spending on luxuries; that was a typical extension.

The use of the trick of extension is surprisingly common. Many people feel that it should be illegal for women to wear full veils (or burqas) in public. An opponent of this position might say that to be consistent if the wearing of the burqa is to be banned, then the wearing of other religious symbols such as crucifixes should also be banned. This might be a reasonable objection if the suggested reason for the banning of the burqa was that it was an Islamic religious symbol. If, however, the supporter of banning the burqa gave as his reason the fact that the wearing of the burqa in public isolated its wearers from other people and this was likely to lead to greater divisions within society, then the reference to religious symbols is an extension of his proposition, which he would be wise not to accept if what he wanted to defend was his original, more limited, statement.

In the same way, the defender of some social change may be met with the argument: 'You suppose that this piece of social reform will produce a perfect society.' The person attacked must reply: 'I don't suppose that it will produce a perfect society, or even that in itself it will solve all our more immediate problems. I only maintain that it will do something to reduce poverty by producing a more just distribution of wealth.' Clearly, if this is true, it is all that the speaker need maintain in order to convince his hearers that the reform is a desirable one. If he were led to make further claims, he would have fallen into the trap of the extension, and would find his proposition more difficult to defend. If he were foolish enough to walk so far into the trap as to maintain that his reform would bring about a perfect social order, his position would become impossible to defend.

Let us return to the attempt to force an extension by saying to one's opponent, 'Logically, you ought to believe that all spending on luxuries is socially undesirable if you think that subsidizing opera is socially undesirable.' This is an example of an old debating trick which deserves special notice – the trick of demanding logical consistency when it is the demand, not the original argument, which is illogical. This trick is not uncommon. If a pacifist argues that it is wrong to take part in a war, he may be told that to be logically consistent he ought to refuse to use violence in any circumstances, even against a criminal who was attacking his wife. This could be a sound argument and not a dishonest trick on one condition, that the pacifist defended his objection to war on grounds that would equally apply to the situation of his wife being attacked. If, however, (as is most likely to be the case) his reasons for not taking part in a war do not preclude protecting his wife from attack, the charge of logical inconsistency is merely a dishonest debating trick. In the First World War conscientious objectors were asked by examining tribunals: 'What would you do if German soldiers came into your house and tried to rape your **** sister?' Apparently the only safe answer was that you would try to get between them. However, if a conscientious objector's opposition to war was based on his refusal to accept violence as an instrument of state policy, rather than to violence under any circumstance, he would have been logically consistent in saying that he would kill the German.

Another common trick in argument is that of the 'diversion'. This is the defence of a proposition by stating another proposition which is not a proof of the first one but which diverts the discussion to another question, generally to one about which the person who makes the diversion feels more certain. One man may say, for example, that the laws in Saudi Arabia preventing women from driving are oppressive to them. His antagonist replies that this is nonsense because it reduces deaths from road accidents. The second statement may or may not be true, but it is not relevant to the first one since obviously the second speaker would not maintain that a country in which the government improves road safety cannot be a country in which the part of its population is oppressed by the laws. That some laws are oppressive to part of a population and that members of this section of the population are prevented from killing themselves in car accidents are two different statements. Either or both of them may be true or false, and the truth or falsity of one implies nothing about the falsity or truth of the other.

This is a diversion because the speaker has shifted the discussion from one topic to another under the appearance of producing an argument for the original topic. Such diversions are found very commonly in arguments; sometimes they are deliberate and sometimes they are unintended. Examples of the use of the diversion can be found in the 'letters' sections of newspapers. Most controversies that are started are not carried to a conclusion because one side or the other creates a diversion in the third or fourth letter. A discussion of the difficulties of controlling football hooliganism may, for example, degenerate in the course of half a dozen letters into an acrimonious squabble about advertising on football shirts or about changes in refereeing. Still more often, it degenerates into a discussion as to which of the two disputants is the more reliable witness or shows the greater respect for 'logic'. Indeed, diversions from any argument to a discussion of personal characteristics of the disputants may be the most common form of diversion. Many disputes end in this way even when they begin with a purely factual problem (such as, for example, which of two vehicles was on the wrong side of the road just before an accident). On-line discussions often degenerate even quicker because of the lack of editorial control.

Another kind of diversion is the trick of fastening on a trivial point in an opponent's argument, defeating him on that, and then leaving it to be supposed that he has been defeated on the main question. A man bringing forward a large number of facts in favour of his case may very well bring forward one, at least, that is not correct. The incorrectness of that fact may not be enough to undermine his conclusion, but an opponent who fastens on the one fact and proves its wrongness can easily create the impression that the whole position of the other is discredited although, in fact, the main support of the argument remains firm. A spurious victory has been gained by a successful diversion. In this case the diversion has not been, as in earlier examples, to a new question but to a side issue of the question under discussion.

There is indeed a danger that any reference to the crooked thinking in an argument may be a diversion from a proper consideration of whether the conclusion of the argument is true or false. A true conclusion, as well as a false one, may be supported by crooked arguments. This does not relieve us of the necessity of examining the arguments to see whether they are sound or not. This is necessary as a preliminary step towards making a judgement as to whether the conclusion of the argument is true or not. But it is only a preliminary; if it is allowed to replace consideration of the truth of the conclusion that is being argued about, it becomes a diversion.

A more impudent form of the same trick is diversion by the use of an 'irrelevant objection'. This is denial of a fact brought forward by a disputant when the truth of this fact is of no importance at all (and not merely of minor importance) to the main argument. A common way in which it is used is to fasten on some detail of one's opponent's case in which he is misinformed. A man may say, for example, that the British claim to the Falkland Islands dates from 1766. His opponent points out that Captain Byron actually claimed the islands in 1765. This is true, but it has no bearing on the argument. A man arguing **67** against the verbal accuracy of the Bible says that he does not believe Jonah was swallowed by a whale. His opponent points out that what is said in the Bible is that Jonah was swallowed by a great fish and that the whale is not a fish. Again true, but irrelevant, since presumably the speaker would find equal difficulty in believing this.

Of course, one ought to be accurate in detail so that one is not open to this kind of irrelevant objection. But we all make mistakes sometimes, and this way of making use of one's opponent's mistakes is dishonest.

Although the weakness of the irrelevant objection is obvious if one thinks about it, this trick is often successfully employed. It is particularly likely to be successful if the objection is of a humorous character. Thus a speaker attacking a shortage of housing may refer to a family of six living in a single room not large enough to swing a cat in. His opponent (or an interrupter) may say: 'Then they shouldn't keep a cat.' It is not a good joke, but it may be a successful diversion because the person against whom it is used is in danger of appearing somewhat ridiculous in his efforts to bring the discussion back to the point from which it is diverted. The audience is more willing to laugh with the person who makes the diversion than to follow the laborious efforts of his opponent to return to seriousness. It is a mean way of trying to win a reputation for being clever, and the person who habitually makes humorous diversions in a serious argument deserves no sympathy.

An example of diversion by irrelevant objection occurred when Mr Gorton was Prime Minister of Australia. He was reported to have said on one occasion that a speech by the leader of the opposition was 'as full of falsehoods as a suet pudding is full of currants.' A newspaper correspondent said that he had consulted an authoritative cook book and found that the recipe for suet pudding showed that it contained no currants. This can be defended as a joke against the Prime Minister who should not have been so careless as to confuse a suet pudding with a plum duff, but as a contribution to the discussion of whether the opposition leader's speech did or did not contain falsehoods, it must be ranked as a diversion by irrelevant objection.

A diversion can, of course, be used by the defender of a position as well as by the person who attacks it. When a man has made a statement and finds himself hard pressed in its defence, he may divert the discussion in a direction more in his favour by substituting for the original statement one that sounds like it but which is easier to defend. Some people habitually begin a discussion by stating an extreme position and then, when this is attacked, they substitute it for a more moderate statement. They thus gain a double advantage. By the original statement they challenge attention and gain an undeserved reputation for being bold thinkers, while the later diversion enables them to escape the crushing defeat in argument which they would otherwise suffer. It is easy for the onlookers to be led to suppose that the original extreme statement is the one that has been successfully defended.

The remedy for all cases of diversion is to bring the discussion back to the question from which it started. This is not, in practice, always an easy thing to do, since an unscrupulous debater will then object that you are evading his argument. With care and good temper, however, it can generally be done.

There is a device related to diversion which we will mention here. That is the trick of bringing in defence of a statement another statement which does not in fact prove it, trusting that one's opponent will not challenge the proof. This can often be ensured by making the supporting statement a reference to a learned theory of which one's opponent will be afraid to confess his ignorance or, at any rate, making the supporting statement in a manner so obscure that one's opponent fears that it would show shameful ignorance if he confessed that he did not see the connection. For example, the theory of evolution by natural selection has been opposed on the ground that it contradicts Third Law of Thermodynamics.

Let us call this method that of the 'inconsequent argument'. The form of the inconsequent argument is simply 'A must be true because of B' when, in fact, A does not follow from B at all. For example, during the 1939–1945 war I heard a propaganda broadcast from Germany in which it was said that Mr Churchill was First Lord of the Admiralty in the 1914–1918 war, and was again occupying the same post in 1939, and that this proved that the war was made by Mr Churchill. This is a completely inconsequent argument, for there is no logical connection between the premise and the conclusion. It is not even to be regarded as a fallacious reasoning process; it is, indeed, not a reasoning process **69** but a verbal device for creating conviction in those willing to be convinced. It is as inconsequent as if I said: 'My neighbour's dog is standing at the door of his house now and he was standing there yesterday morning, which proves that he stole the sausages from my kitchen yesterday afternoon.' Of course, the conclusion might be true, but the argument does nothing to prove that it is true.

An inconsequent argument becomes the starting point of a diversion if it leads the discussion away from the original question to a consideration of a new point that has been brought forward. If, however, the new point is treated as a proof of the original position, there is no diversion; it remains an inconsequent argument.

A completely inconsequent argument is perhaps not often used deliberately. It is rather that those engaged in discussion, when strongly convinced of the position they are defending, are inclined to be careless about the arguments they use in its favour. Inconsequent arguments are fairly common. If an opponent in argument is guilty of one, the remedy is to ask him to explain exactly how his argument proves his conclusion. This is to admit ignorance, and if the argument is not really inconsequent and your opponent can clearly show the connection, he will gain an advantage. If not, however, your profession of ignorance has done you no harm. Too much fear of admitting ignorance lays you open to much crookedness of argument.

Another dishonest argument, used frequently, is to discourage action against some admitted evil by pointing to some other evil which is stated to be worse than the first evil, but about which the user of the argument is making no proposal to do anything. For example, as an argument about attempts to abolish wars, it has been pointed out that more deaths have resulted from road accidents in this country during some number of past years than the total casualties in the Afghanistan war. This would be reasonable grounds for regarding it as important to find out ways of reducing the number of road accidents, but it is a dishonest argument when it is urged as a reason for not trying to bring to an end the Afghanistan war, or whatever war we or our allies may be engaged in at any particular time. The dishonesty of this argument lies in the fact that there is no good reason why we should not try to do both: to prevent people being killed on the roads and also to

prevent them from being killed in wars.

It is a useful argument for the dishonest debater because it can be adapted to a large number of situations. It can be used as an argument against action for the abolition of any evil, for there is no evil so bad that a worse one cannot be found to compare it with. Thus someone may ask why we put money into conserving wildlife when there are starving people in the world. Motorists who are brought into the courts for exceeding the speed limit or for parking offences may argue that the police should not be concerning themselves with such minor matters when old ladies are being battered to death by gangs of thugs. During the time of apartheid in South Africa, when black South Africans had an inferior legal position to whites, there was controversy in Australia as to whether racially segregated sporting teams from South Africa should play matches in Australia. Some of those in favour of their admission argued that those opposing the South African teams were hypocritical because Australian neglect of its aboriginal population was worse than the South African treatment of its African population – a sound argument for improving the treatment of Australian aborigines but not for refraining from protest against racial segregation in sporting teams if one thinks that such segregation is wrong. These may all be considered to be clever debating tricks but are quite unsound when judged as rational argument. The reply to all of them is that if Y is a worse evil than X, this is no reason for not trying to remove X although it is a sound reason for fighting even more energetically against Y.

There is another common trick of argument which seems not generally to be recognized as a trick, so it seems worthwhile to discuss it here. It is the device of presenting one's own view as the mean between two extremes. We all love a compromise, and when someone recommends a position to us as an intermediate one between two extreme positions, we feel a strong tendency to accept it. Knowing this, people of the most diverse opinions present their views to us in this way.

A political canvasser comes to us and points out that the Conservatives represent one extreme in politics and that the Labour Party represents the other, while his party, the Liberal Democratic Party steers a moderate course between these two extremes. We feel, as moderate people, that we must support the Liberal Democrats. **71**

Straight & Crooked Thinking

This faith is a little shaken when the Conservative canvasser calls and points out that the Conservative idea of constitutional liberty is midway between the insanity of the left-wing parties and the thuggishness of the British National Party. We are still further shaken when the Labour canvasser urges us to support a party that steers a middle course between the capitalist parties on the one hand and revolutionary communism on the other. Finally, perhaps, we find ourselves at a Communist meeting where the speaker points out (quite truly) that the Communist party avoids on the one hand the conservatism of the capitalist parties and the bourgeois Socialists and, on the other hand, the chaos of the anarchists who deny the necessity for any organized government at all.

By this time we should sadly have come to the conclusion that the idea that truth lies always in the mean position between two extremes is of no practical use as a criterion for discovering where the truth lies, because every view can be presented as the mean between two extremes.

A second reason for distrusting this piece of crooked thinking is the fact that when we have two extreme positions and a middle one between them, the truth is just as likely to lie on one extreme as in the middle position. If I wished to convince you that two and two make five, I might commend it to you as the safe middle position between the exaggerations on the one hand of the extremists who assert that two and two make four, and on the other hand of those who hold the equally extreme view that two and two make six. I should appeal to you as moderate men and women not to be led away by either of these extreme parties, but to follow with me the safe middle path of asserting that two and two make five. As moderate men and women, perhaps you would believe me, but you and I would both be wrong because the truth would lie with one of the extremes.

Supporters of creationism suggest that teaching the creation story as well as the more conventional theory of evolution provides balance. This is nonsense and was rejected by the courts. It is equivalent to people who believe that the earth is flat insisting on equal time in geography lessons, to put forward their views as well as the idea that the earth is round. Balance is only an argument for dealing equally with two ideas that have equal validity. The issue was whether

72

'Creation Science' is a valid science; if so it should clearly be treated in a balanced way; if not, then 'balance' is irrelevant.

It is not, of course, to be supposed that every representation of a position as a mean between two extremes is necessarily a dishonest argument; it may not be an argument at all. It is a useful teaching device which may be used quite honestly as a means of explaining a position, but not as a way to persuade one's hearers of its truth. If, for example, a lecturer on social psychology wants to explain how much of decent and socialized behaviour in human beings is based on their inborn tendencies, he may contrast Hobbes's view that men are naturally at war with each other and are only kept good citizens by fear, with that of Kropotkin who supposed that instinctively they were altruistic and only became self-seeking by the bad effect of the social organization under which they live in a capitalist society. He may point out objections to both of these views and then develop a middle view that there are both inborn tendencies to socialized behaviour, and inborn anti-social (or criminal) tendencies. He need not say or suggest that this view is true because it is a mean between the views of Hobbes and Kropotkin; he may only have used these views as an aid to making clear what his own position is. Any view can conveniently be explained by comparing it with two sets of views differing from it in opposite directions. It is, however, dangerously easy to slip from this honest use of comparison to the crooked thinking of suggesting that a position ought to be accepted because it is the mean between two extremes.

8

Some logical fallacies

THE DEBATING TRICKS described in the preceding chapter, such as that of suggesting that a statement ought to be believed because it can be expressed as a mean between two extremes, are generally used in an open and undisguised form. There are other faults in reasoning which would be obvious if they were displayed in a simple manner, but which may well be overlooked in the actual course of argument.

Whether the argument is really sound can then often be made clear if we tidy it up and reduce it to a skeleton form, replacing the serious matter of the argument by some trivial matter about which we do not feel strongly or by a mere set of symbols such as A, B and C, about which we have no feelings at all.

For example, suppose that we hear the following argument in a discussion of communism: 'Any society in which the citizens are not free to criticize the government is a bad one, whatever benefits of material prosperity and national unity it may bring its citizens. On this ground we must condemn the communist system of government since in such societies criticism of the government is treated as a crime.'

There are obviously two questions that may be asked about this argument: whether the facts asserted in it are correct, and whether the argument is a sound one in the sense that, if the facts were true, the conclusion would follow. Here we are concerned only with the second of these questions, as to the soundness of the argument. As a step towards judging this, we may simplify the argument to the

form:

> All governments that may not be criticized by their citizens
> are bad.
> A communist government is one that may not be criticized by
> its citizens.
> Therefore, a communist government is bad.

Or we may further simplify the argument by means of a set of symbols in which A stands for the class of governments whose citizens are not free to criticize them, B for the class of bad things, and C for the class of communist governments. The argument is then reduced to the form:

> All As are Bs.
> All Cs are As.
> Therefore, all Cs are Bs.

This is the general structure of a class of familiar and obviously sound arguments. This way of presenting an argument is known as a *syllogism*. If the first two of these statements (the premises) are correct, then the third (the conclusion) rigidly follows.

The soundness of the argument can be made even clearer if we represent it by a diagram in which the large outside circle represents B (the class of bad things), the smaller circle inside it represents A (the class of governments not allowing criticism by their citizens) and the small black circle in the middle represents the class of communist governments.

Figure 1 • *Sound syllogism*

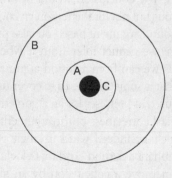

The situation stated in the argument that all governments of the A kind are bad is represented on the diagram by the circle A being **75**

wholly included within the circle B; and the situation that all communist governments are of the A kind is shown by the small black circle C being wholly inside the circle A. It evidently follows that the C circle must be wholly inside B, so all communist governments must be bad. Other people might, of course, use this argument with a different C: instead of 'communist government', it might be 'military dictatorship', or 'fascist government', or C might be the government of some particular country.

When we say that an argument is sound, we mean no more than that it is in a logically correct form, and that if the premises are true the conclusion necessarily is also true. This obviously is not enough to ensure that the conclusion is true; we must also know that the statements contained in the premises are correct. For example, we might construct such an argument as the following:

> *All fungi are poisonous.*
> *Mushrooms are fungi.*
> *Therefore, mushrooms are poisonous.*

This is a sound argument but, although it is correct in logical form, the premise is false, since of course not all fungi are poisonous. An argument of correct logical form based on false premises can lead either to a true or to a false conclusion. We might have made the above argument lead to a true conclusion while still based on a false premise by substituting 'death-caps' for 'mushrooms' in the second and third lines. The conclusion would now be true, death-caps are indeed poisonous but not for the reason given. It is still the case, however, that the sound argument based on false premises does not prove the conclusion: we cannot infer from it whether the conclusion is true or false, as we can from a sound argument with true premises. One method that is sometimes used to cover up false or doubtful facts that are being used as premises for an argument is to draw attention to the formal logical correctness of the argument in question. Someone using this trick may indeed wind up their very dubious argument with the triumphant assertion 'And that's logic!'

If we cannot prove a conclusion by an argument which is correct in its logical form but is based on false premises, it is also true
that we cannot prove a conclusion by an unsound form of argument

based on true premises. Let us, for example, consider the following argument:

> The delusions which mislead men arise from their tendency to believe that to be true which corresponds to their wishes. One of the strong desires that affects human belief is the hope that they will escape extinction at death and live eternally in some ideal haven of bliss. No one who has any understanding of the origin of delusional systems in human wishes can fail to conclude that this belief in immortality is a delusion.

Again, we may be uncertain whether or not this is a sound argument both because it deals with a matter on which we are inclined to feel strongly and also because the structure of the argument is concealed by a lot of words. But, if we reduce it to a simple form it becomes:

> *Delusions are beliefs in what we wish to be true.*
> *Belief in immortality is a belief in what we wish to be true.*
> *Therefore, belief in immortality is a delusion.*

Or, in A, B, C symbolism:

> *All As are B.*
> *C is a B.*
> *Therefore, C is an A.*

That this argument is unsound is clear if we replace it by a trivial example with true premises which lead to an obviously false conclusion.

> *All cats are four-legged animals.*
> *All dogs are four-legged animals.*
> *Therefore, all dogs are cats.*

The unsoundness of this form of argument becomes apparent if we try to draw a diagram for it like that given in Figure 1. We should have to put the circle representing A inside the circle representing B, but all we should know about the circle representing C is that it must be somewhere inside the big circle B; it might be either inside or outside the smaller circle A and it could fit any of the four models in Figure 2. In other words, the conclusion might be true or false. **77**

Figure 2 • *Unsound syllogism*

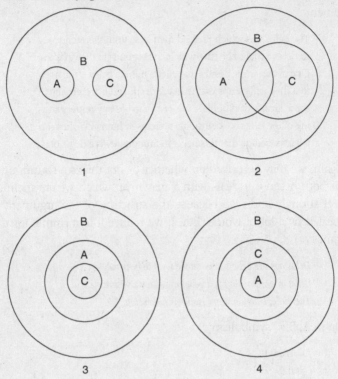

This particular form of crooked thinking is called 'the fallacy of the undistributed middle'. It has this name because the term common to both premises, the 'middle term' B, is not completely covered by either of the other two terms. That is, in both premises the word omitted before B is 'some' and not 'all'. It is plainly not the case that all beliefs in things that we wish to be true are delusions; some are and some are not. We wish when we go to bed to be alive and well when we wake up the next morning and most generally we are; we may also wish that we shall win a prize on a lottery ticket we hold and most generally we do not. If we believe that we are sure to win, that belief will be a delusion. If the first premise in the above argument had been that all beliefs founded on what we wish to be true were delusions, the argument would be logically sound but its first premise would be false. As has already been pointed out, a conclusion derived from an argument in correct logical form with false premises is no more to be relied on than is a conclusion derived from faulty logic. The most that can properly be concluded from the facts put forward in this argument is that belief in immortality may be a delusion. If one wants to decide whether it is or not, it must be from other considerations than the fact that the belief coincides with our wishes.

Arguments of this type are not as uncommon as one might suppose. Naturally they are on matters on which feeling is strong, and generally they are not expressed in such a simple form that the process is apparent. But this kind of implied argument is found: 'The so-called moderate Socialists are only disguised Marxists. They want to transfer industry from private hands to the state. That is what the Marxists did in the Soviet Union.' Or, alternatively: 'The capitalist governments of Great Britain and the USA are fascist. The fascist government of Germany was anti-Marxist, and so are the present governments of Great Britain and the USA.' Both of these arguments and all others of the same type are examples of the fallacy of the undistributed middle.

It is perhaps most commonly met with in propaganda against an individual who supports a cause not approved by the more conventional elements of public opinion; one, for example, who takes a leading part in opposition to a war in which his country is engaged. The propaganda against such an individual may take some such form as this: 'Dr S is constantly criticizing the part played by our country in the present war. Opposition to the war is one of the planks of Muslim extremist propaganda. So it is evident that Dr S is in reality a Muslim extremist.' Reduction of this argument to a skeleton form shows that it too is a fallacy of the same type. What is stated in the premises is not inconsistent with there also being non-Muslim extremist critics of the war, or with Dr S being one of these. The conclusion 'that Dr S is in reality a Muslim extremist' is, therefore, not proved. This kind of an argument is often known as 'damning by association'.

The first step necessary to enable us to detect logical fallacies in argument is that we should get out of the habit of judging the soundness of an argument by considering whether we agree with its conclusion, and concentrate instead on examining its form. Since often the form is obscured by the way the argument is presented, and since also we are inclined to overlook unsoundness of form if the subject-matter **79** of the argument is one on which we feel strongly, it is well to form the habit of putting arguments about which we are doubtful into a skeleton form with A B C symbolism. When we have done that we should be able to see at once whether the argument is sound or not.

The syllogism is an old form of skeleton argument and it is often convenient to use, but it is not the only one available. Let us consider another way of achieving the same end.

The beginning of many arguments can be reduced to the form of statement that if P is true of some particular X, then Q is also true of X. The argument given earlier on in this chapter, for example, may be expressed in the form: if a government can't be criticized by its citizens, then that government is a bad one. P (that it can't be criticized by its citizens) is true of a communist government, so it follows that Q (it is a bad one) is also true of a communist government. Obviously the conclusion follows soundly from what goes before: if it is agreed that any government that can't be criticized by its citizens is a bad one, and that a communist government can't be criticized by its citizens, then it cannot be denied that a communist government is bad.

Another conclusion that can legitimately be drawn from 'If P, then Q' is that for any particular for which Q is false, P also must be false; if the government of any country is a good one, it must be the case that that government is one that allows criticism of itself by its citizens.

In other words, from the fact that if P is true then Q is true (that P implies Q), we can draw two sound conclusions:

1 That for anything of which P is true, Q must also be true.
2 That for anything of which Q is false, P must also be false.

There are also two fallacious conclusions that might erroneously be drawn from the fact that if P is true, then Q is true. These are:

(a) That for anything of which Q is true, P must also be true. From knowing that the government of a country was a bad one, we could not conclude that its citizens were not free to criticize it; other features of a government may make it bad as well as restrictions on its citizens' freedom to criticize it.

(b) That for anything for which P is false, Q must also be false. Knowing its citizens were free to criticize the government, we could not safely conclude that the government was a good one; it might be or it might not be.

When we say that the last two conclusions are fallacious, we do not mean that they are necessarily false, only that their truth does not follow from what has gone before; they may be true or false. That they are fallacious is perhaps best made clear by a simple example in which the conclusion is obviously false. There is no doubt that being an elephant implies having a trunk. To infer from this that any animal with a trunk must be an elephant would be a fallacy of type (a). The conclusion is obviously wrong since a tapir also has a trunk. To infer from the above statement that any animal not an elephant has no trunk would be a fallacy of type (b); it also is refuted by the fact that the tapir has a trunk.

At this level of simplicity this may all seem self-evident. It may be by no means self-evident in the more complicated kinds of argument in which these fallacies do actually occur. For dealing with these more complicated arguments the method of reduction to a skeleton form is a useful testing tool. The argument, for example, that Dr S must be a Muslim extremist because he opposes a war which the Muslim extremists also oppose can be reduced to the form of the fallacious argument (b): if P implies Q then Q implies P. In this case:

> *Being a Muslim extremist implies opposition to the war.*
> *So opposition to the war implies being a Muslim extremist.*

The conclusion that Dr S must be a Muslim extremist because he is opposed to the war no more necessarily follows than does the conclusion that the tapir is an elephant. The other examples given to illustrate the fallacy of the undistributed middle may also be treated in this way.

There is thus more than one way of reducing an argument to a form in which its soundness or unsoundness becomes apparent. We can use either or both of the methods described. We must choose the way that best serves the purpose of making clear to ourselves and to those we have discussions with, which of the arguments used are sound and which unsound.

I should not wish the above discussion of logical forms to lead readers to buy an elementary textbook on logic and start learning **81**

by heart the sound and unsound forms of the syllogism. That might
be useful for passing an examination in logic, but not for learning to
detect and avoid mistakes in reasoning. What is to be learned from
logic for this purpose is, I would suggest, its techniques of reducing
arguments to a skeleton form. When this has been done, we should
be able to see directly whether the arguments are sound or not. If
we are still in doubt, we can try various subject matters for the arguments and see whether they lead invariably to true conclusions. If
they sometimes lead to true conclusions and sometimes to false, the
form of the arguments must be unsound.

Before ending this chapter I should mention two fallacious
arguments that are well known – the argument in a circle and the
argument which begs the question about which the dispute is taking
place. These are somewhat less common in adult controversy than
the fallacies that have been already mentioned, but they are found
sufficiently often to be worth a short examination.

The general form of the argument in a circle is: 'P is true because
of Q; Q is true because of P.' It is sometimes argued, for example,
that human action is not free because what happens in a choice
between two actions (let us say, between running away and standing
one's ground in danger) is that the stronger impulse (to stand one's
ground, for example) overcomes the other. If we further ask how we
know that the impulse to stand one's ground was the stronger, the
reply is that it must be so because that is the behaviour which actually took place. The argument then reduces to the form: the impulse
to stand still overcame the impulse to run away because it was the
stronger impulse because it overcame the other – an entirely circular
movement.

We have already (in Chapter 1) mentioned the crooked argument
by 'begging the question' or assuming what is to be proved (for instance, by saying 'this scoundrel who drove his wife to her grave').
This cannot be done blatantly: if one began an argument by stating
as an agreed principle the point that was in dispute, the trick would
be too transparent to be successful. It can, however, be done by
using a form of words that implies the conclusion, although not in an
obvious way. The example given in Chapter 1 of the use of words in-
82 volving moral judgement when a moral question is at issue is a fairly

transparent trick, but it is not uncommon as an important part of a complicated argument. If a disputant wants to establish the guilt of an individual or a group, he is likely to use an argument in which he describes them as 'criminals', 'villains', etc.

Another method of using the same trick is to assume what has to be proved in a definition. In order that this trick may be used, it is not necessary that formal definition of the words used should take place. The question-begging definition may only be implied.

Let us suppose that A and B dispute as to whether Christians lead better lives than those who are not Christians. A maintains that they do, but in opposition to him B points to numerous people who go to church and profess Christian beliefs but who drink too much, neglect their families, and lead otherwise discreditable lives. A, however, refuses to accept this as evidence against his contention on the ground that those who do such things are 'not really' Christians. A's argument implies a definition of Christians which includes, as one of the essential marks, the leading of a virtuous life. The question in dispute is begged by A's implied definition of a Christian.

Clearly one can prove a large number of propositions by a similar method. One could prove that all swans are white by refusing to count as a swan any bird that was not white (including black swans in Australia). Some people are unwilling to admit that this is a crooked argument. They may argue that the word 'Christian' is used in various ways and that a definition which includes the leading of a virtuous life as one of the essential marks of a Christian is not unusual and quite legitimate, and if the definition be accepted, then the conclusion cannot be denied. This is true, and if the statement that all Christians lead virtuous lives is taken simply as a statement of how we are going to use the word 'Christian', no important objection can be made against it. In the argument given above, however, disputant A meant more than a statement about how he used words: he certainly meant to state a proposition about outside fact. This proposition was that those who possessed the external marks of being Christians (going to church, professing the Christian creed, etc.) also tended to possess the character of leading a virtuous life. This may well be true, but it cannot be established by the argument which A used, for he begged the question at issue by his definition.

Argument in a circle and begging the question are universally recognized as dishonest tricks in argument. In order to refute an opponent who uses one of them, it is therefore only necessary to show that the trick is being used. In order to do this it is sometimes necessary to put one's opponent's arguments in a simpler form so that the error may be more easily seen. This is certainly the case when the question has been begged by choice of words or by definition.

9

Habits of thought

THERE ARE FORCES within our own minds that tend to produce crooked thinking. Two of these are our habits of thought and our prejudices. These are two different forces of a somewhat similar kind. I am using the term 'habits of thought' for those directions which our thoughts normally and habitually take, and 'prejudices' for those ways of thinking that are predetermined by strong emotional forces in their favour, and by real or supposed self-interest. Both habits of thought and prejudices may be exploited in similar ways.

The formation of habits of thought is part of the familiar process of habit-formation in our lives. Our daily life is largely directed by habitual ways of behaving; we get up, eat breakfast, and go to work in much the same way every day. Such habit-formation has the value of economizing effort; choice is arduous and may conveniently be reserved for decisions of importance. The same is true with respect to our ways of thinking and forming opinions. When we read our newspapers or watch the news on television, we hear about cuts in government spending, about internal discord within countries, about differences of opinion between governments and so on. We have most likely made up our minds about the rights and wrongs of all of these problems before (or we have had our minds made up for us) so we need not form new opinions about them. Our thought-habits avoid the necessity for making new decisions on the controversial issues underlying these news reports. This economizing of intellectual effort is a principal advantage of having formed thought-habits.

There are, on the other hand, at least two grave disadvantages of thought-habits. First, knowledge of the hearers' thought-habits can be **85** used as a weapon by a speaker. Secondly, thought-habits may close our minds to new ideas.

The public speaker who wishes to exploit the thought-habits of his hearers will generally know enough about his audience to find no great difficulty in starting off his speech with some statements that exactly fit those thought-habits. He knows when he has succeeded in doing this by the applause that follows. A skilful orator may begin his speech with a succession of such statements. He refers to 'the British traditions of justice and fair play' (applause), to 'the democratic spirit of the British people' (more applause), and to 'the hardworking families who are the backbone of our nation' (still more applause). By this time he has produced in his audience an attitude of willingness to accept what he says. He can now go on to say things which earlier their thought-habits would have led them to reject. He can say, for example, that we are spending too much money on the armed forces, or that immigrants are all scroungers. And the audience is likely to go on accepting what he says. The resistance which would certainly have been shown against these statements if he had started with them has been broken down by this simple device of beginning with easily accepted statements.

The same device may be used by a faith healer. He tells his audience that the mind has great power over the body, which is true. He goes on to illustrate this power by recounting stories which may also be true. He may tell, for example, of people who seemed to be dumb or paralysed who became suddenly well under the influence of some emotional crisis. He may even illustrate this power by some simple experiments. When his audience is in a receptive state of mind he goes on to tell them other things which, without this preparation, they would have found less easy to believe. He may tell them that he has a new method by which all their illnesses, physical and mental, may be cured; this method will be communicated to small groups on payment of a fee. If the device of softening-up by preliminary appeal to habits of thought has succeeded, the members of the audience will have gone on believing the speaker when he has made these unsupported claims because the first things he said seemed to them to be obviously true.

So if we hear a succession of statements A, B, C and D, which our minds accept readily and with enthusiasm, we must still be on our

guard against accepting a fifth statement, E. A, B, C and D may only have been ground-bait intended to produce the habit of swallowing everything the speaker says; E may conceal the hook.

Our caution, however, should extend even further than this. The ease and readiness with which we accept A, B, C and D is no guarantee that even they are true. Thoughts we have often thought pass through our minds with increasing ease until they appear obvious. Emotions that have been called up in connection with particular thoughts are aroused more easily by those thoughts until the connection between emotion and thought appears to us to be a necessary one. So it is not correct what we cannot doubt must be true. What we cannot doubt may simply be based on a very deeply rooted thought-habit and may well be false.

Our ancestors, for example, found themselves unable to doubt that the earth stood still while the sun moved around it every day. Yet this conviction was wrong, and was based simply on deeply grounded habits of thought. This set of thought-habits was broken by Copernicus when he showed that the facts were better explained by supposing that instead of the sun moving around the earth, the earth rotated on its axis.

We all of us tend to judge problems from one particular standpoint – the one determined by our conditions of life. We are inhabitants of our own particular country, with a particular religious and moral tradition, and we are inclined to forget how many of our judgements are simply relative to this single standpoint and are not absolute.

It is only when we begin to study comparative religions and comparative codes of morals that we begin to see to what extent our own opinions about right and wrong and about other matters are not objective truths (for these are true for all persons under all conditions), but are judgements whose truth is relative to the particular point of view from which they were made. By forming the habit of trying to look at problems in a manner which is independent from our own point of view, we can to some extent escape from this relativity.

There is a story of many years ago about the captain of a British warship who was commissioned to visit a South Sea island and to make a report on the manners and customs of its inhabitants. His report is said to have been along the lines of: 'The inhabitants of this **87** island have no manners; as for their customs, they are beastly.' It is not difficult to see that this is not an objective account but one that is relative to the system of manners and customs the captain was accustomed to. It might be reworded: 'Neither the manners nor the customs of the islanders were such as I should expect on my own ship.' A modern anthropologist would probably have discovered that the islanders had a very elaborate code of manners, and he would have recorded their customs as fact, without concerning himself with the question of which of them he liked and which he did not.

When people visit foreign countries, their reports are often of the same kind as this captain's: 'The Chinese eat strange foods', or 'The Germans have no sense of humour.' Objectively considered, all these are statements in relation to our own customs as a frame of reference. The first states (truly or falsely) that the Chinese eat different foods from those the speaker is used to. The second means either that the German people laugh less than the traveller does, or (more probably) that they laugh at different things.

Political and social systems of foreign countries can also be unfairly judged from our own point of view. Citizens of European and North American countries have been brought up in a tradition which places great value on the rights and aspirations of individuals; they may thus regard democracy as the only acceptable political system. In other parts of the world social cohesion and the individual's place within a harmonious society may be much more important than his freedom to do and say what pleases him. Many African countries are artificial creations imposed by the colonial powers, in which different ethnic groups are trying to find a sense of nationhood. In such countries Western-style democracy may simply result in the despotism caused by one group's domination of another. Yet we often insist that the only worthwhile system for all these countries is 'first past the post' democracy, and much of our foreign policy is directed towards making other countries more democratic. It may well be that what is more important in these countries is an effective legal system to protect the rights of the individual, rather than a democratic electoral system. We should not be too keen to impose our own political ideals on countries that are different in many respects from our own.

Our attitude to international politics is also affected by our point of view. If there were a dispute between, let us say, Bolivia and Peru, most of us would be able to judge its merits, if we had a sufficient knowledge of the facts, in an objective manner. If the dispute is, however, between our own and some other country, we can no longer do so. Until we can see and feel the other side's case as well as our own, our judgements cannot possibly even approach objective validity. Most people seem not to realize this, and after a war we suppose that we and our allies are capable of acting not merely as prosecuting attorneys against our late enemies, but also as their judges. Now, a judge has to make objective, universally true judgements, and this could plainly only be done by someone as detached from our dispute as we should be from one between Bolivia and Peru.

An instructive experiment is to take a statement expressing our own point of view on a subject on which we have well-developed habits of thought; then, making no other alteration, to change the particular subject to another which is similar but about which we have different thought-habits. Now we can consider the statement with its new subject-matter and see whether our attitude towards it remains the same. So we judge how far our attitude towards the original statement possessed objective validity, and how far it was acceptable to us merely because it fitted in with our thought-habits.

We may try this experiment with the following imaginary speech being given to volunteers going out to teach English in the nation of Ruritania.

> When you go to Ruritania, remember that you are going not just as a teacher but also as an ambassador for the values that the English people hold dear. You are bringing with you not just the English language that is the immortal heritage of Shakespeare and Dickens, but also you will carry with you the English love of freedom that is enshrined in our parliamentary system and has come down to us from the Magna Carta. The English have been the standard bearers of Western civilization throughout the world for many years. It is your duty to uphold our values and by example instil into the Ruritanian people the spirit of democracy.

This is a very patriotic speech but it is not difficult to identify with the sentiments expressed and to feel admiration for the high motives invoked. To test the real worth of the passage we will try it again in a setting in which we have formed different habits.

Let us imagine a speech given in the same circumstances in the Soviet Union before the fall of communism.

> When you go to Ruritania, remember that you are going not just as a teacher but also as an ambassador for the values that the Russian people hold dear. You are bringing with you not just the Russian language that is the immortal heritage of Chekhov, of Tolstoy and of Pushkin, but also you will carry with you the Russian love of freedom that is enshrined in our Party system and has come down to us from the authors of the Communist Manifesto. The Russians have been the standard bearers of Marxism throughout the world for many years. It is your duty to uphold our values and by example instil into the Ruritanian people the spirit of Communism and the brotherhood of man.

That is the same passage as before in a different setting. The setting has been changed to one in which we have different thought-habits. Our reaction, too, is different. Instead of a dignified statement of national responsibility, it sounds as if it is being given to KGB recruiting agents. How would the original passage have sounded to an impartial visitor from Mars?

One of the most important ways in which failure to see the situation from any other point of view than one's own may have disastrous consequences is in the genesis of quarrels. When these quarrels are on an international scale they may result in the catastrophe of war. In some respects their mode of origin may not be very different from the more trivial quarrels between individuals.

Let us suppose that Mr Jones finds the cat of his neighbour Mr Robinson scratching up the seedbeds in his garden. He writes a note of protest to Mr Robinson. Mr Robinson resents the note and sends a hostile reply. Mr Jones is still more annoyed by this and puts wire-netting between the gardens, fastening it to the fence (which happens to be the property of Mr Robinson). Mr Robinson is angered by this disfigurement of his fence and cuts the wire-netting off. Mr Jones then sues Mr Robinson for damage to his wire-netting, while Mr Robinson sues Mr Jones for damage to his fence.

We now have a fully developed quarrel. The point of view of each participant is that his neighbour became aggressive on trivial grounds while he himself merely took action to protect himself. If the disputants appeal to us, as impartial onlookers, to decide which was the aggressor, we shall find it difficult to decide. We may prefer to say that both have found themselves in a peculiar situation in which their mutual hostility is intensified by each step taken. We may also judge that both are to blame because the grounds of the quarrel were so trivial that either might properly have broken the chain of increasing instability by refusing to take the defensive step which provoked the next defensive step taken by his neighbour. If such a quarrel had started in the nursery it would probably have been settled before it went very far by both antagonists being told off and sent to bed.

A parallel situation may arise between two nations. Nation X may fear the danger of war with nation Y, so X decides to increase the strength of its armed forces. Y sees in this a threat to its security and increases its own armed forces. X is confirmed in its impression that Y intends to make war and increases its own forces, also making a treaty for mutual defence with a neighbouring country, Z. Y is now sure of X's aggressive intention and feels that it is beginning to be encircled by enemies, so it buys more tanks and aircraft and makes alliances with its neighbours so that it can have additional forces for its protection, new airfields, etc. At the same time, the statesmen of both nations assure the world of their sincere desire for peace and their reluctance to engage in war preparations in order to protect themselves against the aggressive intentions of the other nation.

From the point of view of X, the position is simply that Y is preparing for war and that they are merely taking steps to defend themselves. From the point of view of Y, X is threatening war while they themselves are preparing to resist X's aggression. From the point of view of a neutral observer, the situation may be parallel to that of Mr Jones and Mr Robinson, that both find themselves in a peculiar situation in which any defensive step taken by either is interpreted by the other as a threat, itself leading to another step of the same kind, which in its turn is regarded as a threat.

The situation is one of increasing instability, which at any point may really precipitate a war. The unstable position may indeed be upset early in the process if either X or Y, being convinced that the other nation intends to have a war at some time, also feels that the chance of their own defeat will be greater next year than now, so the war had better start now.

Unfortunately the chain of causes leading to war is less easy to break than in the case of Mr Jones and Mr Robinson, for the issue is not a trivial one. If a statesman of X fails to counter what he regards as provocative measures by Y, and if war does nevertheless break out between them, a heavy weight of blame will rest on him for not having taken steps necessary to guard against the defeat of his country. It may be argued that it is better that he should risk defeat rather than risk war. This may be true; it must obviously depend partly on the relative seriousness of the two risks, and that is a difficult matter for him to judge. He has to weigh against each other the danger that he may provoke war by defensive measures which the other side regards as provocative and that he may risk defeat by neglecting those measures.

The pressure of his own nationals is likely to be altogether on the side of taking the measures which seem provocative to Y, because his people (and he himself) will see the situation from the point of view of his own nation X, which regards X as desiring peace and Y as aggressive. It is only if the statesmen and people of both X and Y can break their own habits of thought and see the problem from the point of view of the other nation as well as their own that such a dangerous set of causes leading to war can be broken.

If states of hostility between nations are more difficult to bring to an end than those between neighbours quarrelling about their pets, it is also more necessary that they should be ended. So those who try to look at international tensions while standing aside from their own national interests are doing a real service to mankind. International misunderstanding is continually being intensified by patriotic talk and oratory on both sides of every pair of quarrelling nations.

The development of a capacity for thinking objectively about the problems of other nations would give us a better protection against war than that provided by the increased fear of war through the making of more deadly weapons.

This is one field in which the questioning of our habits of thought may lead to a clearer insight into the true nature of a situation, and may increase the chance of our behaviour being reasonable. In general, our thought-habits should not be passively accepted but should be subjected to critical scrutiny. Even the things about which we feel most certain are likely to have been questioned by someone, and it may not be a bad thing for us to hear these questionings, so that our deepest beliefs may be based on reasoned and critical conviction and not merely on thought-habits. One may, for example, profitably read newspapers and books representing a political point of view that is not one's own. A Christian believer may read what is said against Christianity by its critics. Believers in climate change should read carefully what is written by its opponents. One whose political thought is inclined to socialism may read what is said on the other side by the conservative press or by speakers of the right.

These will all experience the uncomfortable sensation of having their long-held and deeply ingrained thought-habits shaken. Their opinions may not be reversed, but they will no longer be merely based on thought-habits that have never been questioned. They will be something stronger and better, the reasoned convictions of free minds. Those whose attitude towards what they regard as subversive literature and speech is simply that it must be suppressed (by force if necessary) show little faith in the reasonableness of the beliefs they are so anxious to protect.

We have in ordinary speech a word for the unpleasant feelings that are aroused in us when something presented to us breaks across cherished mental habits. We say we are 'shocked'; and we resent being shocked. Many people believe in a censorship of writing, films and programmes which will save them from any danger of being shocked. They avoid reading books or going to plays which may shock them. Those of our grandparents who were most tender to their thought-habits avoided reading such authors as D. H. Lawrence and Bernard Shaw because they thought that these authors were deliberately trying to shock them. They do not seem particularly shocking to us, because they succeeded in their aim of shaking people's thought-habits so well that the ideas they suggested are no longer startling, but familiar. Some seem to us to be true and some false, but they can all be thought about and talked about without any discomfort.

We can also profit by reading more modern authors who seem at first sight to be merely perversely questioning what every sensible person knows to be true. Such writers do us a great service, of forcing us to question our old beliefs, so that we may freely and intelligently choose what is sound in them and reject the rest, and thus have our minds prepared for seeing new and unfamiliar truths. Most people do not need protection from being shocked. They need to be shocked a great deal more than they are.

This is probably more generally recognized now than it was when *Straight & Crooked Thinking* was first written. At any rate, now there is more writing that is considered to be shocking than there was early in the last century, and the implied questioning of generally accepted habits of thought is more thorough-going than it used to be. It is, however, still the case that those who value settled ways of thinking exert pressure for censorship of the more shocking kinds of literature, plays or films. What is considered shocking is very different now. Whereas in the last century most of the cultural taboos were concerned with sexual behaviour, religion, bad language, and to a lesser extent, violence; now the main issues are the desire not to cause offence to people on the grounds of their gender, religion, race or sexual orientation. There can, of course, be a reasonable case for prohibiting some publications but not on the ground that they would shock some readers. A better ground for preventing the publication of a book is that the reading of it would lead to evil behaviour. Whether or not this would be the result of reading a particular book or viewing a particular film is not easy to judge, and the grounds on which it would be judged are different from those that would be used for determining whether it is shocking.

The value of shocking ideas lies in the fact that there are a number of problems about which most people have so many habits of thought that they resent any questioning of them. 'Does Islam condone some kinds of violence?'; 'Should homosexuality be discouraged by the **94** education system?'; 'How much inequality is good for a country?'

These are all questions which when merely raised in public set in action thought-habits connected with such strong emotions that reasonable discussion and reasonable decision are quite impossible. Yet there should be no question reasonable people dare not ask, no thought so shocking that we cannot consider it long enough to make a sensible decision as to whether it is true or false.

We must not suppose that we have escaped the danger of being imprisoned by our thought-habits merely by giving up our old habits of thought that are much the same as everybody else's and starting new ones of our own. The unorthodox and unconventional are in just as much danger of finding their minds closed to new truth by the persistence of their old habits of thought as are the orthodox and the conventional. They too have just the same need of being occasionally shaken out of their thought-habits so that they may retain flexibility of mind.

A danger which threatens those who have rejected commonly accepted habits of thought is that they form the habit of disbelieving things merely because other people believe them. They then become what are commonly called 'cranks'. A crank is not an individual free from thought-habits, but one who has formed a system of thought-habits that is likely to be as hampering to him as is the opposite system of accepting all that is commonly believed.

It should be one of the aims of education to produce a quality that we may describe as 'flexibility of mind', an ability to try out new ways of thinking and to make unfamiliar assumptions. This means that we must be able at will to put on one side our old thought-habits. So we must keep for ourselves the power of intellectual experimentation. We see everywhere people carrying out work for wages. We must ask ourselves: 'Is this a necessary law, or can we imagine a form of society in which the monetary motive would not be the dominant one and yet in which the world's work would be done?' We are accustomed to a particular form of marriage relationship. We should ask ourselves: 'Is this the only one possible? Would other kinds of relationship be better or worse in securing the ends for which marriage exists?' We have probably been brought up in a particular religious tradition whose teachings may seem to us to be self-evidently true. It may, nevertheless, be profitable to try the experiment of thinking ourselves **95** into some other system of religious beliefs, so that we can go some way towards seeing with the eyes and hearts of those holding a different system of beliefs, which may not be merely those of some other Christian denomination but perhaps of some other religion, such as Buddhism or Islam. Such an exercise may not change our own beliefs; it should change our attitude towards those who hold other systems of belief.

Clearly it is neither desirable nor possible to get rid of all thought-habits. The formation of thought-habits is as inevitable as the formation of bodily habits and just as useful. But we must be ready continually to revise them. Thought-habits once serviceable may prevent us from attaining to new truths. We differ from the lower animals in the possession of a rich and complicated brain. This is an instrument to give flexibility and adaptability to our behaviour. If we allow ourselves merely to become creatures of habit, we become automatic and mechanical like the lower animals. We are allowing our brains to degenerate into mere mechanisms when they were meant for plasticity and change.

Astronomers tell us that the human race has many millions of years more to spend on this globe if it does not destroy itself by war, environmental pollution, or unrestricted population growth. It is only by flexibility of mind that we can continue to adapt ourselves to an ever-changing environment. Inflexibility of mind may lead to the extermination of the human race.

10
Prejudice

HABITS OF THOUGHT are not the only factors that predispose us to crooked thinking. There are also our prejudices, already defined as ways of thinking that are predetermined by strong emotional forces such as those derived from our own self-interest. These may have the effect of making us unwilling to think straight on certain topics. Someone with no formal knowledge of logic may come to quite correct conclusions on a question such as the relative chances of drawing a red or a black card from a complete pack, where the facts are simple and the reasoning perfectly straightforward. On the other hand, the learned author of a textbook on logic may be quite unable to come to reasonable conclusions on a question in which his own interests are deeply involved – for example, job security for university lecturers.

Education does not in itself save us from this disability. It ought to help us towards freedom from prejudice, but it does not necessarily do so. Learned academics are often as bound by their prejudices as anyone else. Learned persons may defend their most unreasonable prejudices by arguments in a correct logical form, while the uneducated defend theirs by illogical arguments. The only advantage this gives the learned is the fact that they can marshal formally correct arguments in defence of their errors. This may make these more watertight against opposing arguments and opposing experience. Mastery of the art of thought may simply make unreasonable opinions more unassailable.

Of course, you, being free from your opponent's prejudices, may see the flaw in their reasons for holding their opinions, but this flaw may very well not be in the form of their arguments. It may lie in what they assume, or in what facts they select of all possible facts to consider. I do not wish to suggest that correct thinking on correct facts can lead to error, but only that there are other routes to error than lack of logic, and the most logical mind guided by its prejudices can and will find its way to error by one of these other routes.

Paranoiac delusions are a particular type of mental disorder. Some people with these delusions think that there is a conspiracy against them, but others have a different kind of belief; for instance, that they are actually someone who is long dead. If we meet a paranoiac and discuss with him his belief that he is a reincarnation of Napoleon, of Julius Caesar, or of Jesus Christ, we do not find a loss of reasoning power. On the contrary, he reasons most persistently about the very subject of his delusions, and the quality of his reasoning is determined by his intellectual abilities. If he has a keen logical intellect he will reason keenly and logically. He will apply the same standard of reasoning in defence of his delusion as he would apply to the defence of his sane opinions, if he were sane. This standard may be high; it may be low. Even sane people often have a somewhat low standard of reasoning. Ask the average man in the street why he believes that the world is round; he is likely to give you a set of very bad reasons. Ask the believer in the delusion that the earth is flat why he holds this belief, and he will probably give you a much better set, for his reasoning powers have been sharpened in continual arguments with people holding the orthodox view. Yet he is wrong, and the illogical man in the street is right. (Some readers may find the references to 'right' and 'wrong' at odds with the current post modernist, relativistic, multicultural world. However, some beliefs, such as that the world is flat, are wrong in most normal senses of the word. Despite the modern world's aversion to the objective 'right' and 'wrong', I see no reason to avoid the use of these words altogether.)

The man with wrong opinions does not necessarily reason poorly. In the same way, the person suffering from insane delusions may show no loss of reasoning power. His defect is that the opinions he holds are very badly wrong, and that his reasoning is used to support these wrong opinions and not to criticize them. Their source is not **98** reasonable. They form a kind of super-prejudice.

When any of us hold the kind of opinions we have called 'prejudices', part of our mind is in a similar state to that of the delusional system of the insane. We too reason to the best of our ability in defence of our prejudices, but these reasonings are not the real support for our opinions. They are based on other (often quite irrational) grounds.

If we argue directly against the false beliefs of a person suffering from delusional insanity, we shall find our arguments unable to shake his beliefs, because they are not directed against the real causes of those beliefs. Our more successful arguments may have a dangerous result, for they may produce an explosion of violent anger. The deep-seated system of emotions protected so carefully by the set of false beliefs will also be protected by anger and physical violence if the protective system of beliefs is in any way threatened.

The same is true to a lesser degree of the opinions of a sane person grounded on emotional or practical needs. He will not willingly allow those beliefs so necessary to his mental comfort to be overthrown, and if our arguments begin to threaten them he will grow angry or at least peevish. When he begins to show anger instead of reasonable opposition to our arguments, we may press home our advantage, for this is an indication that his beliefs are beginning to be threatened by our arguments.

This use of an opponent's signs of anger as an indication that we have touched what he feels to be a weak spot in his argument is, of course, a perfectly legitimate device in argument. There is also a dishonest trick that may be used in connection with the anger of an opponent. This is the trick of deliberately angering him to take advantage of the fact that he will argue less effectively when he is angry. This we may do, not only by pressing on a weak point in his argument, but also by adopting a deliberately insulting manner, by making fun of matters on which he obviously feels strongly, or by the use of such irritating tricks as diversion by irrelevant objection.

Knowledge of the nature of this trick and of its purpose makes the remedy obvious. We must always be determined that nothing shall make us angry in discussion, because, however annoying our opponent may be, we shall best defeat him by keeping our temper under control. If we feel anger rising, this should be a signal to be increasingly courteous to our opponent and increasingly critical of our **99** own position. We can also use the first stirrings of anger to detect the weaknesses of our own position.

In brief, we may express the effect of prejudice on opinion by saying that we are inclined to believe what we either desire or need to be true and to disbelieve what we desire or need to be false. If we have put our last pound on a horse running at 100–1, we fervently believe that it will win and we shall reject the view of a friend that it is a hopeless case and is likely to come in last, if it finishes at all. Similarly, if a man is suffering from a dangerous illness he may refuse to believe that his illness can really be fatal because his desire for life makes him unwilling to accept the evidence that he is unlikely to recover.

Sometimes it is obvious how the emotions that determine our acceptance of some propositions and rejection of others came into existence. Almost everybody desires money and comfort, and fears ruin and death, so they will tend to accept ideas whose truth would secure their wealth, comfort and security of living, and reject those whose truth would threaten them.

Sometimes, however, the connection between emotions and prejudices is more obscure. The emotion lying behind a prejudice may be a relic of the emotional life of early childhood. Our childish love for our father or our resentment against his discipline may be the determining cause of our adult reverence for authority or of our rebellion against it. Which of these two factors was the stronger in our childhood may thus determine whether we shall be monarchists or republicans, conservatives or revolutionaries. Similarly, our sympathy with oppressed peoples may be based on our childhood fantasies of rescuing our mother from distress.

Whether the connection between the prejudice and the emotion giving rise to it seems obvious (as in the case of political opinion determined by the amount of a person's possessions), or obscure (as in the case of opinions determined by his childhood relationship to his father), recognition of this connection may not be possible for the holder of the prejudice. It is the essential nature of a prejudice that the connection should not be apparent. The prejudiced person believes that he holds his opinion on entirely rational grounds. If he understood that his opinion was really based on irrational grounds, his prejudice would disappear. He might still hold his former opinion or he might reject it, but if he held it, it would have to be on grounds other than those on which it was based when it was a prejudice. The strength of the prejudice depends on the fact that he cannot become aware of these irrational grounds on which it is based. The further these grounds are hidden from his awareness, the more strongly is the prejudice held.

Let us suppose that two men are arguing about a proposal to increase death duties. One of them is in favour of the increased tax. He argues the case in its favour entirely on general grounds, with logical arguments as to its general economic effects. His opponent argues hotly against it with equally general arguments. Neither of them argues the question from any consideration of how the proposal would affect him personally, and both would indignantly reject the suggestion that the effect of the levy on themselves plays any part in determining their opinions about it. Yet, as onlookers, we are not surprised to learn that the man arguing for the levy is an orphan, while the man arguing against it has a rich, elderly father. Nor are we likely to be wrong in guessing that these facts are much more important influences in determining the opinions of the two men than any of the logical arguments they bring forward so impressively.

Or we may look at the newspaper correspondence about a proposal to put a holding centre for asylum seekers or a rehabilitation centre for drug addicts in the residential district of Linden Avenue. Most of the letters that are critical of the proposal will find fault with it on general grounds: that the traffic along Linden Avenue would be hazardous for people from the Sahel who are not used to cars, or that it would be dangerous for the children of Linden Avenue to have drug addicts in their neighbourhood. Other letters may support the proposal on the grounds that it is good for new arrivals in the country to be in a pleasant district, rather than in a city centre, or that the respectable environment of Linden Avenue is ideal for the rehabilitation of drug addicts. None mentions personal reasons for objecting to or supporting the proposal, but when we look at the addresses from which the letters are written, we find that most of those objecting to the proposal are from people living on or near Linden Avenue, while the letters supporting the proposal come from other districts. We may well guess that the question of **101** how much the writers of the letters will be personally affected by the proposal is a more important factor in determining their attitude towards it than the more general considerations which they bring forward as arguments.

We must not, however, make the mistake of supposing that, when opinions based quite irrationally on people's personal desires or repugnance are bolstered up by apparently reasonable arguments, this is simply hypocrisy in the ordinary sense. The holder of such an opinion is generally quite unconscious of the irrational grounds of his belief and honestly believes that his reasonable arguments are the real grounds for his belief. He would be genuinely indignant if it were suggested that his opinions on the question under dispute had anything to do with a consideration of how he himself would be affected. The true reasons for his belief are hidden from his consciousness. He is not a hypocrite; he is merely a self-deceiver.

Such a rational bolstering up of a belief held on irrational grounds has been called a 'rationalization'. When our desires lead us to believe something, our minds construct a rational set of reasons for supposing that belief to be true. The belief does not, however, follow from the reasons; the reasons follow from the belief. They are mere 'rationalizations' of a belief really held on irrational grounds. A sufficiently ingenious mind can rationalize any belief, however absurd. Some people can produce rationalizations for the belief that Stonehenge was built by aliens, others for the belief that the apparent location of star constellations at your birth determines your fate, while others will argue that water has a memory that allows homeopathic preparations to work without any of the active substance being present, or that the moon-landings did not actually take place. The capacity of many people to deceive themselves by rationalization is a formidable barrier to straight thinking.

There are many other beliefs of this kind, intermediate between the delusional systems of the paranoiac and the prejudices of the normal person. The holders of such views are not usually insane. They are abnormal in the fact that they hold these opinions with an irrational degree of certainty and that they show unusual imperviousness to opposing evidence. In these respects they resemble true paranoiacs

but in other respects they do not. Such systems of thought may be

Prejudice

called 'paranoid' systems, using the termination …*oid* to indicate that they are *like* paranoiac delusions.

If paranoid systems were only concerned with such topics as the influence of aliens on prehistoric architecture, they would be of no great practical importance, although they would remain interesting as illustrations of the strength of the irrational forces in human minds. They become serious when they take a form resembling a paranoiac's delusion of persecution. The typical form of such a paranoid system is: 'There is an enemy "X". He is cunning, powerful and wicked and his aim is to destroy our civilization. He is responsible for drug addiction, sexual perversion, strikes, student demonstrations and wars.' The unknown 'X' may be identified with some known group or it may be left somewhat vague. 'X' may be identified with the Jews, Al Qaeda, the Freemasons, Opus Dei, the Knights Templar, or any combination of these. The mode of operation of 'X' may be regarded as through a widespread though secret conspiracy.

A good example of such a paranoid system in which 'X' was identified with the Jews is to be found in Hitler's *Mein Kampf,* which is now far enough away in time to be looked at objectively. One can recognize its quality of persuasiveness, which led to widespread acceptance of its point of view in Hitler's country. Yet the grounds for its theory of a Jewish plot is no more than unsupported assertion in emotionally charged language. The alleged details of the plot were derived from a book called *The Protocols of the Elders of Zion* which is known to be a forgery. It is possible, of course, that Hitler himself was insane, a true paranoiac. But the paranoid system he evolved was accepted by millions of sane people, and this acceptance produced terrible damage to the world and its peace.

The development of paranoid systems of thought involving imagined persecution did not end with Hitler. In our own culture the enemy 'X' in such a system was for a while Saddam Hussein, who was believed by some to be responsible for terrorist activities around the world despite the lack of evidence linking him to these attacks.

It is desirable that those who value a rational approach to political, racial and religious questions should be able to recognize the character of such paranoid propaganda when they meet it. For this purpose some understanding of the nature of paranoid systems is useful. **103**

There are, of course, reasonable arguments against the communist system of government and reasonable objections to the way the CIA carries out its business. But these reasonable cases are not promoted by delusions of communist plots, or CIA-backed conspiracies, which are part of crooked thinking and interfere with a rational assessment of the real issues.

One characteristic of our mind that leads us into paranoid systems of thought is our desire to make sense of a confused world. Our minds are constantly looking for patterns, focusing on facts and ideas that fit into these patterns and subconsciously rejecting those that do not fit in. We are impressed by coincidences and remember them easily, forgetting times when they do not occur. Similarly information that fits into our preconceived world view is more readily remembered than other information. In extreme forms this tendency leads to conspiracy theories, where everything that is not readily explained is fitted into a single theory about sinister forces controlling the world.

Since it is an essential character of prejudice that its sources are hidden from consciousness, it might seem to be impossible for us to become aware of our own prejudices so that we may become free from their influence. It is hopeless to try to do so by looking inside our own minds and trusting that we shall be able to recognize our prejudices. Their source is hidden from our own consciousness and they will look to us just like rational beliefs. But we can learn to recognize them in another way – by applying to our own opinions the same criteria that we apply when we see prejudice in other people. If we see another person holding opinions that correspond to his or her wishes we suspect that these opinions are prejudices, and if we notice ourselves holding opinions that correspond to our own wishes we have equally good grounds for suspecting prejudice. If we find ourselves getting angry when some cherished belief is questioned, we may suspect that such belief is a prejudice based on irrational grounds just as we would if we observed someone else getting unreasonably touchy about an opinion. We are not likely to understand fully the irrational sources of our opinions, but we can have some knowledge of them if we examine our own opinions as **104** critically and unsympathetically as we do the opinions of others.

It is perhaps even more useful to keep a general awareness of the fact that we are likely to have prejudices and to adopt methods of counteracting their influence. One such influence, for example, is that they may lead us to overlook faulty thinking in writings or speeches we agree with, while they enable us readily to detect errors in what we disagree with. So, in all matters in which our emotions are strongly involved (either for or against), we must distrust our own judgements and compare them carefully with those of people who disagree with us. Our prejudices tend also to make us forget facts unfavourable to our opinions. Darwin records that he kept a notebook in which he jotted all facts or ideas that were opposed to his conclusions, because otherwise he forgot them. So when he published his results, his opponents could bring forward few objections that he had not already considered.

Prejudice has two other important effects. It distorts one's memory and it may incline one to accept as true ideas that are not supported by facts. One must be particularly cautious in quoting from memory any evidence in favour of a view one holds. I have frequently typed from an apparently vivid memory incidents recorded in books I had read, but on examining the books again I have found the original passages were somewhat different from that which I had quoted and were generally less favourable to the view I was trying to support. Serious errors of fact have crept in this way into books whose authors have not sufficiently realized how much memory may be distorted by prejudices. In some cases these distortions are not important, but sometimes they may alter the entire sense of what has been said. Many misremembered or misattributed quotations have become widely accepted, because they have the ring of authenticity. For example, the Nazi leader Goering never said 'Whenever I hear the word culture I reach for my revolver' – this is actually a line from a play, but it sounds like something he might have said. There is a famous speech attributed to the Native American Chief Seattle in 1854, in which he pleads for respect for nature, including such memorable phrases as 'The Earth is our Mother.' This has been widely used as an inspirational text by the environmental movement. Unfortunately the most widely quoted parts of this speech were written for a Hollywood film in the 1970s, and there is considerable doubt about the contents of **105** the historical speech. We are most inclined to believe things that fit with our existing world view, have a ring of plausibility and are heard often. If they have an element of humour they may be more readily remembered, and then believed.

Both false quotations and outright falsehoods are easier to accept with frequent repetition. The internet has increased the tendency of people to believe things that are simply not true, since a single falsehood can be widely circulated, and come to people from many different sources, giving the appearance that it is widely accepted.

There is a common fault in argument arising from the influence of prejudice, which may be employed deliberately as a dishonest trick but which is more commonly used unwittingly by a speaker who is misled by his prejudices. This is the use in one context of an argument which would not be admitted in another context where it would lead to the opposite conclusion. This is 'special pleading'.

There are many examples of this; for instance, a bishop who was actively engaged in trying to increase the pay of poorly paid vicars rebuked the coalminers for wanting a pay rise because 'a pound a week more wages does not mean a pound a week more happiness.' People living off inherited wealth are heard to deplore the sapping of the will to work by the payments of insurance benefits to unemployed workers. The construction of nuclear submarines is sometimes defended simply on the ground that it makes work – an argument that could equally well be used in defence of building roads in excess of requirements, making men shovel sand from one point of our shore to another, or even (as Bernard Shaw pointed out) as an encouragement to motorists to knock down pedestrians. Obviously there can be reasonable arguments against an increase of miners' wages and against the payment of unemployment benefits, or in favour of the building of more submarines, but any such arguments can only be accepted if the principle on which they rest is valid in other particular cases as well as in the one under consideration.

In arguments about wages and salaries, some arguments are consistently applied in one context and some in another. Company directors resist wage rises for their workers because of their inflationary tendency, but they do not use this as an argument against
increases of directors' fees which are also inflationary in their effect.

Wealthier people may argue that it is a good thing that they should have a large income because: (a) the amount they save is reinvested into the economy, or (b) the amount they spend, even on luxuries, is good for trade and increases employment. They may also argue that the wages of manual workers should be kept at a moderate level because: (c) more pay for workers causes inflation, (d) there would be no incentive for workers to better themselves if they were already highly paid, and (e) if the workers were paid more, they would only spend it on useless luxuries and alcoholic drinks. There is obviously much special pleading here. Points (b) and (e) are inconsistent with one another; the view that luxury expenditure is socially valuable is applied to one class of the community while the view that it is a social evil is applied to another. Point (a) also is not applied to the manual workers, while (c) and (d) are not applied to the group to which the speaker himself belongs. We may further ask whether the person who argues in this way really believes (a) and (e), which imply that the thing of greatest social value to do with money is to save it, or (b) which implies that the right thing is to spend it on no matter what. It is useless to ask which he believes. He believes in both propositions and will employ either in different contexts. People have a much greater power of believing inconsistent propositions than is commonly supposed.

The obvious way to deal with special pleading is to get the person using this device to admit the general principle that underlies their particular argument and then to apply it to the particular cases they have ignored. Politicians often object to tariffs imposed on imported goods by other countries since they say that it interferes with free trade. One would need to ask the politician who was saying this whether all interference with free trade was a bad thing. If he admitted this it could lead to the further question whether he would therefore be opposed to subsidies paid to his own farmers since this also interferes with free trade by making it more difficult for imported food to be competitively priced.

In trying to detect and undermine special pleading, one must be careful not to do one's opponent the injustice of attributing to him an extension (see Chapter 7) of his proposition. In the above case, for example, the speaker may not have intended to imply that **107** all interference with free trade was a bad thing, but only when the interference was in trade in manufactured goods, rather than food-stuffs. We must allow him to tell us what the general proposition is that he is prepared to defend, and then attack it either by making other particular applications which he will reject, or by showing its untruth in some other way.

Knowledge of the prejudices of his audience can, of course, be used by an orator in exactly the same way as knowledge of their habits of thought. He can make easier the acceptance of a doubtful proposition by wording it in such a way as to make it appeal to the prejudices of his audience, or by introducing it only after the statement of a number of other propositions enthusiastically favoured by their prejudices. These devices and the methods of dealing with them are essentially the same as have already been described in the chapter on thought-habits (Chapter 9), so they need not be dealt with here.

There is, however, a particular form of the first of these two devices that deserves fuller mention. That is the trick of commending or condemning a course of action because of its good or bad practical effects on the lives of one's hearers. A very considerable part of political propaganda is made up of this kind of appeal. Whether attacking national expenditure on the armed forces or on social services, a speaker can get a ready response by pointing to its effects in increased taxation. Our objection to increased taxation is primarily a very individual and personal one, that as we pay more in taxes we have less to spend on ourselves and our families. Even when the speaker makes a relatively impersonal basis to the appeal by emphasizing the effect of high taxation as a burden on industry, we can safely guess that it is the effect on themselves that the audience is thinking about. That is likely to be the true reason for the success of the speaker in carrying conviction.

Yet each person in the audience could, if they were sufficiently detached emotionally from their own affairs, truthfully reflect that its effect on them is not a wise basis for deciding on national policy. Somebody without children might feel that spending on education does not benefit him, but that does not affect its importance for the country as a whole. In fact, he will not reason like this; an appeal to an audience to welcome with patriotic fervour a lowering of their own standard of living because this will benefit the nation as a whole will fall very flat. It is a peculiarity of the sentiment of patriotism that people can be more easily persuaded to sacrifice their lives for their country than to sacrifice the contents of their pockets.

When people realize how many of their opinions and even of the reasoning processes by which these are supported are based on known or unknown emotional foundations, they may begin to doubt whether they can believe anything at all. This doubt is, of course, absurd. There must be sound opinions even on questions about which the strength of our own feelings makes it most difficult to discover which they are. One way of distributing wealth can be better than another, and rational thought can help to discover which is that better way, even though his own possession or non-possession of wealth is likely to be the strongest influence in determining a particular individual's opinion as to which is the better way. Similarly, there must be an objectively true answer to the question whether at death we just disappear like candles blown out or whether we continue our conscious existence for all eternity. Yet which of us (whether believers or disbelievers in personal immortality) will suppose that he holds his opinions on the matter on grounds that are scientific and objective, and independent of his own feelings and desires?

The attitude of detachment of mind is one that can be cultivated and must be cultivated if we are to arrive at true conclusions on matters which touch us personally. The first step is to recognize the existence of this kind of irrational motivation in our own minds; then we can make allowances for it. If we are rich, we must try to force ourselves to think out social problems on general grounds without allowing ourselves to be influenced by our own powerful desire for the continuance of our individual comfort and security. Whatever our personal circumstances may be, we must learn to adopt the same attitude towards the sorrows and pleasures of others as we do towards our own, and to adopt the same attitude towards our own sorrows and pleasures as we do towards those of other people. Of course, that is hard, much harder to do than to say. So we must always be prepared to admit that our conclusions as to what is best for others may have really been dictated to us by consideration of what is best for ourselves. But we can and must do our best to detach ourselves from our **109** own irrational motivations of opinion. The first step in that detachment is to recognize them.

Nor must we make the foolish mistake of supposing that we can settle controversies by attributing prejudices to our opponents and by labelling their arguments 'rationalization'. Some people seem to think that it is a sufficient argument against socialism to say that it is based on the envy of those without possessions for those with, and that its intellectual defence is just a rationalization of this envy. This is no more reasonable than the opposite argument that conservatism is merely based on the determination of the wealthy to hang on to what they have got, and that its intellectual defence is simply a rationalization of this determination. Undoubtedly the desire of the poor for wealth and of the wealthy to hold on to their money are powerful motive forces behind the belief in socialism and in capitalism respectively. But having made all allowances for the strength of whichever of these prejudices our own circumstances have given us, the question remains – which is the better system? That is a question we cannot settle by discussing the prejudices of our opponents. A true opinion as well as a false one may owe much of its strength to irrational motives.

11

Predigested thinking

SOME OF THE forms of crooked thinking that have been discussed result from a feature of much human thinking, which it will be worthwhile now to describe and name. Most true statements about complicated matters of fact cannot be adequately expressed in a few words. To give an account of the effect of diet or climate on health or of the effect of an increase in wages on the level of inflation would require many words, many qualifications, many distinctions between different cases, and many uncertainties. Most people, however, are impatient with these complications. They feel that they have mastered the matter when they can reduce such a complicated question to a simple formula with all the qualifications, distinctions and uncertainties left out.

There have been great arguments in many countries about whether, and under what conditions, the abortion of human foetuses is morally justified. The difficult and complicated problem of weighing the value of a human life at a very early stage of development against its mother's life, her health or her convenience has been reduced to the phrases 'A woman's right to choose' and 'Protect the unborn child'.

Let us call this tendency 'predigested thinking'. It is a widespread reaction to intellectual difficulties. Darwin's complicated theory of the evolution of life was popularly reduced to the simple formula: 'Survival of the fittest'. Freud's psychoanalytical theory of human emotional development was a highly complicated and difficult set of ideas. This, however, has been simplified to the expression: 'Everything is sex'. In **111** the same way, the difficult mathematical physics of Einstein's theory of relativity may be summed up in the phrase: 'Everything is relative'. What research has discovered about the values of different kinds of food may also be summed up in predigested form as: 'Milk is nourishing', 'Sweets contain calories', and 'White bread is bad for you'.

The tendency to eliminate complications from statements may explain the prevalence of the substitution of 'all' for 'some' (Chapter 6), the ignoring of the undistributed middle (Chapter 8), and the readiness to accept an extension of the position one starts to argue in favour of (Chapter 7). In all these cases, the substituted proposition is the less complicated one, and therefore the one that those under the influence of predigested thinking are liable to accept.

A man may, for example, be arguing against the teachings of Freud. He will almost certainly begin to attack the view that 'everything is sex'. His own tendency to predigested thinking has led him quite unwittingly to invite his opponent into the trap of the extension. His opponent may be better informed on the matter and try to explain which activities Freud thought were related to sex and which he did not. This, however, is of no interest to the first speaker, and he escapes by protesting that his opponent is too 'learned' or too 'subtle' for him. He protests that he is a plain man and that nothing will convince him that art, romantic love and religion are just sex, which as everyone knows was what Freud claimed. Thus he entrenches himself in his predigested thinking, and if the dispute takes place before an audience he can generally be sure of having their sympathy, for his opponent will seem to be trying to make himself out to be too clever and make serious argument impossible by throwing doubt on what everyone knows to be true.

A statement expressed in predigested form has the great practical advantage that it can be easily remembered and easily passed from one person to another. It is, therefore, simple for belief in it to be increased by the force of 'suggestion' (Chapter 13). No kind of suggestion is stronger than the conviction that 'Everybody says so-and-so' and this is the basis of much advertising. Phrases like 'Guinness is good for you' and 'Persil washes whiter' contain little rational inducement to use the products, but are predigested phrases that help people to remember what their qualities are supposed to be.

Predigested thought is also often used as a basis for arguments. Some old sayings are repeated so often that people use them without remembering that they are not necessarily correct or to be applied in all circumstances. One argument that is never honest is the use of the phrase 'the exception that proves the rule'. When a man maintains an extreme position such as that politicians have no honour, he can quite properly be refuted by his opponent pointing to members of the small band of recent politicians who have acted honourably. He may then try to justify his original extreme statement by saying: 'These are the exceptions that prove the rule.'

This is obviously false. It can be dealt with by pointing out (as is self-evident) that exceptions do not prove that a general rule is true but that it is false. His opponent may also point out that the word 'prove' in this old saying originally had the meaning 'test', and that it is true that the way to test a general rule is to look for exceptions to it, whereas it is obviously not the case that finding exceptions 'proves' the rule in the modern sense of showing that the rule is a correct one.

In the same way someone may use phrases such as 'honesty is the best policy', 'charity begins at home', 'there's no smoke without fire', 'a woman's place is in the home', or 'my country, right or wrong', 'the thin end of the wedge' as if they were adequate arguments by themselves. Any use of such a phrase without further justification can be considered dishonest argumentation using predigested thought.

A predigested thought formula expressed in a form of words that is handed from one person to another may be called a 'slogan'. A successful slogan may possess great power in influencing a large number of people to do the same thing. No complicated statement of the doctrines of Rousseau, whose ideas inspired the French Revolution, could have been as effective as the slogan 'Liberty, Equality, Fraternity'. Now, this slogan is obviously predigested. It is a very simple statement that would need a complicated expansion to mean anything exactly. Such an expansion of 'liberty' would need to explain what the people were and what they were not to be free to do; of 'equality', in what respects they were to be equal; of 'fraternity', to explain with whom they were to be fraternal (presumably not aristocrats or enemies of their country). Yet such an expanded account would not serve any of the purposes of the slogan: that it should be readily accepted in its 113 entirety, easily remembered, and able to stimulate a large number of people to similar action.

The use of slogans as a method of influencing people is not necessarily unreasonable. A skilful leader of men, however sophisticated his own ideas, would need to express his doctrines in predigested form for them to be widely accepted and, for the purposes of mass action, this could most conveniently be done by inventing slogans. Thus the Russian Revolution was directed not by preaching the subtleties of Marxist theories to the people, but by the slogan, 'All power to the Soviets.' This can be considered a legitimate use of a slogan; slogans can reasonably and properly be used to stir people to action but not to induce belief.

Probably there is no single explanation of the tendency to accept and respond to predigested thinking. There is the difficulty of grasping a complex proposition. The most finely developed brain eventually reaches the limit of the complexity it can grasp. With the majority of people this limit is reached rather early. Long before it is reached, however, mental idleness steps in, making us tend to accept mental food well below the limits of our digestion. It is easier to believe that Richard III or Hitler were thoroughly bad men than to accept a dispassionate estimate of all the sides of their characters. So, through idleness or indifference, such a predigested opinion is accepted even by those who would be capable of making a more complex judgement if they chose to make the necessary mental effort. As the world gets more complex, even those people who are capable and are willing to make the effort, simply cannot have personal knowledge of all the key issues of the day. Whereas 200 years ago a well-educated person might expect to have some real level of understanding of most important issues; today the world is so complex that it is impossible to have real knowledge of any but a small number of issues. For most of these we may have a rather limited and simplified understanding, which is unlikely to stand up to serious cross-questioning by a real expert.

Because of this we have to accept predigested thinking, since it gives us a consistent practical attitude towards problems in life. During a war, for example, we are inclined to think of our enemies as altogether evil, as treacherous, murderous and inhuman. This view was well expressed by a newspaper correspondent during the Second World War: 'There are no poor dear German people . . . but only a brutalized nation.' If, during a war, someone suggests that there is a mixture of good and bad even in the enemy, or that some of the stories of enemy atrocities may be exaggerated, or that they have sometimes shown generous and human behaviour, he is regarded as a person of doubtful loyalty with a secret sympathy for the enemy cause.

The feeling of outrage aroused by the expression of such an opinion is a result of the fact that it tends to undermine the simplified picture of the enemy as evil. In a war, one is engaged in the practical activity of fighting the enemy and any belief which makes one fight more strenuously is of service. From the same practical point of view any belief which makes one fight less strenuously is undesirable. The conduct of one's enemies, like one's own conduct, is, in fact, a mixture of bad and good. But while belief in the bad strengthens our hands in fighting, belief in the good side of our enemies' characters would weaken our efforts. So we accept the over-simplified picture of our enemies as evil because that is the most useful picture for action, not because it is true.

It is not only in wars and revolutions that one finds the kind of thinking in which all perfection tends to be attributed to one's own side and all evil to the enemy. In elections it is very noticeable; while the candidates on one side appear as models of all the civic and domestic virtues, those on the other are regarded as incompetent and untrustworthy persons. Here too action is required, and action must be simple, however complicated the thought leading to it. One must vote on one side or the other; so to avoid being crippled by doubt the mind tends to pile up certainties in one direction in the form of over-simplified estimates of the characters of the two parties.

Our attitude to sport is often the same. Members of the team we support are clean-living and high-minded, and if they indulge in acts of violence on the field this is only the result of a natural excess of high spirits. Members of the opposing team are at best a bunch of mindless automatons, while at worst they are drug-crazed maniacs with no idea of fair play. Our side either triumphs gloriously or is deprived of victory because of cheating by the opposition, partisan refereeing or the effects of foreign food. Such reasons never explain the other team's defeat.

This biased way of seeing things is understandable. We are likely to have read in the newspapers and seen on television details of the private lives of the sportsmen and women from our own country and to be aware of the various difficulties they have had to overcome to achieve success. This makes it much easier to identify with them than with the anonymous sportsmen from other countries. Also it is only by identifying completely with one side that we can find a sporting event really interesting, since much of the pleasure is lost if we realize that winning or losing matters equally to both sides. While there are competitive sports it is unlikely that these habits of thought can be eradicated. Provided that it is remembered that the outcome of sporting events is not really of great importance in the world, no great harm is done. When this is forgotten, people may not just be partisan supporters of their own side and attribute all virtues to them, but may also harbour active feelings of antagonism towards the opposing team and their supporters. Football hooliganism is the most obvious result of this kind of attitude.

In spite of all the hard things which may justly be said against predigested thinking, its service to action is of importance. Our enthusiasm for straight thinking must not blind us to the fact that what we do is more important than what we think. We must act effectively, even though we may be too clever to fall into the snare of predigested thinking. If we do not accept predigested thinking as a stimulus to effective action, we must learn to act effectively without it. So important is action that we can reasonably condemn as crooked thinking any kind of thought that has the effect of evading useful or necessary action. 'There is much to be said on both sides, so I shall do nothing about it', is a common type of thinking of those who are too intelligent to fall into the pitfall of popular predigested thinking, and it is itself a pitfall just as dangerous. Let us call it academic detachment from practical life.

There is, in politics, much to be said for conservatism, much for socialism and much for whatever falls between the two. But if we realize this so fully that we do not cast a vote at all, we are doing less than our neighbours who see less clearly than ourselves. Something is going to happen as a result of the poll, and the effect of our abstention from voting is as likely to affect the result in an undesirable way as any of the three possibilities of voting. By not voting we have not really escaped from the requirement of playing a part in the election; we have only made it impossible that our part will be a useful one.

We cannot escape the necessity for action, and our conviction that there is much to be said on all sides does not absolve us from the necessity for acting vigorously and effectively on the side on which we think the truest and wisest things are said. If we are driving a car across an open space and an obstacle appears in front of us, we can avoid it by going to the left or to the right. The arguments for both may be about equally balanced. We must, however, do either one or the other wholeheartedly without allowing the excellent case for the other side to affect our action. If we are content to say that there is much to be said in favour of both sides and drive straight on, we shall be in danger of breaking our necks.

The path of wisdom is to act in an effective and wholehearted manner on the side that seems to us, on the whole, to be the best. Realization of all that can be said on the other side should make us tolerant of those opposed to us and ready to revise our courses of action under the influence of new evidence, but it must not be allowed to interfere with the effectiveness of our action in the direction that we have calmly and clear-sightedly chosen. We must steer a middle course between the whirlpool of predigested thinking and the rock of academic detachment.

Although predigested thinking may have some practical usefulness, it is obviously a hindrance to straight thinking. If truth, and not idleness or convenience, is our aim, we must always beware of it. Even though predigested thinking is narrowly useful in providing motives for strenuous action, there is a wider sense in which its results are highly dangerous.

12

Pitfalls in analogy

I N THE COURSE of explaining any complex and perhaps abstract matter, it is an advantage to use a concrete illustration in order to make one's meaning clear. A climate scientist, for example, trying to explain the effect of carbon dioxide on climate, may compare this situation with a blanket that absorbs heat and prevents it from being radiated again. Such illustrations are a common and useful device in explanation. A mental picture can often be easier to understand than an explanation in words.

The scientist giving this illustration may be merely intending to give a vivid picture of an abstract matter so that his hearers are able to grasp the theory he is trying to explain; he does not intend his analogy to create in his hearers a conviction of the truth of that theory. When, on the other hand, a concrete illustration is used to create conviction of the truth of whatever it illustrates, or when it implies that truth in order to deduce some new conclusions, it is no longer a mere illustration; it is then an *argument from analogy*.

After the international financial crisis of 2008 some critics of the banking system said that one of the major causes was allowing banks to act like casinos owned by utility companies. The analogy here is that part of what banks do – taking deposits and lending money – is essential to the day-to-day functioning of the whole economy, and is a necessary function within society that is equivalent to utilities such as electricity and water supply. However, banks were not only providing these services, they were also speculating on subprime mortgages and

the like. The suggestion here is that the situation was like an essential utility such as a water company being closely linked to a highly risky business like a casino; it was suggested that the solution was to ensure that banks could not carry out both types of activity.

Although this analogy may seem a compelling argument, on looking more deeply into it we see that there are vital differences between the two cases that make the analogy worthless. Casinos are actually very safe businesses. They work on a clear understanding of the nature of risk, and on well-defined margins. The risk associated with many rolls of a die is very low, and even if a punter occasionally makes a big win, this is never more than the casino has factored in already. The real parallel would be not with the casino, but with an individual gambler who may be risking his entire wealth on a single hand of cards. Thus what is contended may well be true, but it certainly cannot be proved by this argument.

People have objected to the democratic election of Members of Parliament or of Congress saying that children are incapable of electing their own teachers, so why should ordinary people be able to select their leaders? Again, however, the analogy is obviously imperfect. Adult men and women are presumed to know more about the qualities required of an efficient ruler than children know about those of a good teacher. Moreover, governing and teaching are such very different functions that a method of selection serviceable in the one case may not be in the other. In addition, the democratic selection of those who govern us partly serves to assure us that our rulers do not act only in their own interest; no similar problem is supposed to arise with teachers. In fact there is so little analogy between the selection of teachers and a parliamentary election that no conclusion can usefully be drawn by analogy from one to the other, whatever other weighty and reasonable objections may be urged against democracy.

The use of analogy in thought or communication is not necessarily wrong, although an argument based on analogy always needs critical examination. Analogy is the way in which much of our thinking is guided; when we meet an unfamiliar situation that we do not understand, we try to think of something familiar which resembles it and to use that as a guide to the new situation. What happens in the familiar case is what we expect to happen in the unfamiliar one, and very generally this expectation is fulfilled. So analogy proves itself a **119** reasonably good guide to conduct; it becomes dangerous, however, when the conclusions to which it points are regarded as certain and not merely as probable.

Reduced to its bare bones, the argument from analogy has the form that because some thing or event N has the properties a and b which belong to M, it must have the property c which also belongs to M. Displayed like this, the argument does not sound a very convincing one.

Things that are alike in some respects differ in others. It may be that a and b are properties in which M and N resemble one another, while c is a property in which M differs from N. A whale resembles a fish in the general shape of its body and the fact that it lives in water. If we knew no better, an argument from analogy would lead us erroneously to suppose that the whale also resembled a fish in breathing with gills instead of lungs. There is a well-known principle in arguing from analogy that we can only safely argue from the possession of one set of characteristics to another if there is a causal connection between them. Even this principle would not, however, save us from error here, because the possession of gills is causally connected with the fact of living in water. This just happens to be a characteristic in which whales differ from fishes.

There is a particular case of analogy which has been called the 'appeal to nature'. Right-wing Christians encouraged people to watch the film *The March of the Penguins* because this showed Emperor penguins demonstrating monogamy and selfless parenting. In broad terms this is the assumption that what is natural is right. Therefore if one sees something happening in nature one may presume that it is morally right. The 'appeal to nature' has particularly been used in discussions of homosexuality and cloning. People who believe that homosexuality is natural and therefore good, look for evidence that it is widespread among wild animals, while their opponents try to demonstrate that it is unusual or only occurs under particular social circumstances. The Nazis made use of Konrad Lorenz's work on animal behaviour, in which he showed that aggression was widespread amongst wild animals, to suggest that it was natural (and therefore right) for the strong to dominate the weak. There are two problems with this approach. One is that even if a particular type of behaviour is natural for a range of animals, this does not mean that it is natural for humans. The second is that even if something is 'natural' for humans, it still may not be morally right. It has, after all, been argued that much of what is worthwhile in human civilization is there to provide restraints to natural and dangerous behaviour. Incidentally the analogy of the Emperor penguins is a poor one in any case, since rates of 'divorce' are higher than those of humans (as with the mute swan, long admired as a symbol of devotion and fidelity).

An argument by analogy is not always expanded into a clearly recognizable form. When a writer refers to 'the keen edge of a man's intellect' or to 'filling the mind of the child with facts', an analogy is implied, in the one case between an intellect and a knife or sword, in the other between a mind and a bucket, bag or box. Such an analogy, implied by the choice of words but not definitely expressed, is a *metaphor*. A metaphor may be used merely for the purpose of illustration, but if (whether purposely or not) the user of a metaphor draws any conclusions from the implied analogy, then he is using the argument from analogy although in a somewhat disguised form. If, for example, one said: 'The keen edge of the intellect will be blunted by frequent use', one would be using a metaphor as the basis for an argument by analogy. The argument would be a weak one since the opposite conclusion would have been drawn if one had paired the intellect with the bodily muscles, which become more efficient through frequent use and become atrophied if they are not used.

In the same way one may hear the mind of a child compared with a container, which may be filled with facts and ideas as a milk jug can be filled with milk. The implication of this comparison is that, like a milk jug, the mind has a limited capacity for facts and ideas and that when a certain number are acquired, there will be no room for more. This conclusion depends, however, on the arbitrary choice of an analogy. One might have thought of the child's mind as a kind of organization in which the more facts and ideas it contains, the more connections there will be for introducing new ones. That would be a different analogy which would lead to different practical consequences. The question as to which is the more appropriate analogy and which is the better guide to educational practice cannot be settled merely by examination of the analogies themselves; it must be discovered by research into the facts of the child's acquisition of knowledge. The original analogy is useful **121** as a guide as to what we may look for in this research; the choice of analogies cannot be taken as a sure guide as to what we shall find in it.

That analogy can be a useful guide to thought is shown by the large part it has played in the development of science. Many of the conceptions that have guided scientific theory have been analogies from familiar objects. Thus atoms and electrons were thought of and treated as if they were tiny fragments of solid matter, and light was treated as waves on a pond. The success with which the science of physics used these conceptions to build up a consistent body of knowledge, and to predict facts which turned out on investigation to be true led to a mistaken trust in the analogies that had been used. It led even to forgetfulness of the fact that these mechanical principles were analogies and not direct descriptions of physical realities.

Yet a point was reached at which these analogies broke down. There were properties of electrons that were not conceivably those of lumps of matter however small, and it was found that in some ways light also behaved as if it consisted of small particles.

So physical theory has turned away from such concrete analogies and expressed its theories by means of mathematical equations. By doing this it has become incomprehensible to most of us, for we feel that we can only comprehend what we can think of in terms drawn from what we can see and handle; that is, by analogies with the outside world of reasonably large objects. Such analogies, however, do not help us to grasp a four-dimensional space-time system or to get hold of the ideas of quantum mechanics. We feel that we must think of atoms as tiny bits of matter or not think about them at all.

The fact that many of the analogies used in the early development of physics broke down in the end does not mean that the using of them was a mistake that held up the growth of true ideas in science. The physical analogies were, on the contrary, an important guide to scientific thought at the time when they were in use. It was by the use of the analogies as guides to observation that it became clear in what respects they were inappropriate. It was only those who clung to the old analogies after they had been shown to be inappropriate who held up the growth of science. The analogies themselves were a means by which science advanced, but they were a means that had to be discarded when no longer useful.

There is a general principle that analogies may be a useful guide as to what facts to look for, but they are never final evidence as to what the facts are. If those who compared banks to a combination of utility company and casino were using the analogy to indicate one possible way to look at the issue, this could be accepted as a useful first step in considering a complicated matter. The next step is to examine the analogy for its appropriateness. In this case the analogy is false, and it must be discarded. But the realization of the inappropriateness is also a step towards understanding the matter under discussion. Someone else may think of a better analogy which may also be examined for its appropriateness. This is all part of a possibly fruitful discussion which may lead to a better understanding of the matter.

That the use of analogy is a possible manner of productive thinking is suggested by its history. It was used as a main method of discussion by the wise men of ancient China. One of these (Hui Tzu) is reported on one occasion to have been told by his king to say things plainly and not to use analogies. He replied that this would be impossible since explaining is necessarily a process of making intelligible what is not known by comparing it with what is known.

An example of the old Chinese use of analogy is to be found in an argument between Mencius and Kao Tzu as to whether human nature is basically good or whether it is neither bad nor good. Kao Tzu said: 'Human nature does not show any preference for good or bad just as water does not show any preference for either east or west.' Mencius replied: 'It is certainly the case that water does not show any preference for either east or west, but does it show the same indifference to high and low? ... There is no man who is not good; there is no water that does not flow downwards.'

Here it should be noticed that although a certain conclusion can be inferred from an analogy, this is not accepted as, in itself, a sufficient reason for accepting that conclusion as correct. Mencius points out that a slightly different analogy would lead to an altogether different conclusion. It is, in fact, necessary to examine the appropriateness of the analogy that has been used.

These are examples where analogy is serving a justifiable purpose. The use of analogy, however, becomes crooked argumentation when it is used not as a guide to expectations but as a proof of a conclusion; **123** not to see how well the analogy fits the facts but as in itself a proof that a certain conclusion is true. Let us call this an *argument by mere analogy*. Of course, the conclusion of such an argument may happen to be true because the expectation aroused by the analogy may happen to be fulfilled. It remains the case that the analogy is not sufficient proof of the conclusion.

Although it is apparent that an argument from mere analogy is not logically a sound ground for belief, it does seem to be a very effective way of inducing belief. This property of inducing belief is a concern of psychology rather than of logic. It seems to be the case that any analogy (good, imperfect, or obviously absurd) tends to produce conviction of the truth of what is asserted in the same immediate and unreasoning way as does a good slogan. If a speaker puts forward an argument in the form 'A is B, just as C is D' (where A and B are abstract or controversial while C and D are concrete and familiar), then his hearers will tend to believe that A is really B without considering how close the analogy is between A/B and C/D. If the relationship between C and D can be clearly pictured in the hearer's mind, this seems to make the process of conviction easier, although this may not be essential to it; the mere fact that the argument is in the form of an analogy is often enough to produce immediate acceptance.

If, for example, a lecturer on alternative medicine says that a positive attitude will remove disease from our bodies just as a policeman will remove a burglar, his audience may be more strongly convinced of the truth of his statement than they would have been by the mere assertion that a positive attitude will remove disease from our bodies without any supporting analogy. Here the analogy is a very imperfect one; the resemblance between a positive attitude removing disease and a policeman removing a burglar is not even close enough to create reasonable expectation, still less to constitute proof. An opponent might say that mere attitude can no more remove disease than can dreaming about a policeman remove a burglar. Although the analogy is imperfect, however, it may be effective in producing conviction simply because it is an analogy. The mental picture of a policeman removing a burglar may be sufficient to produce belief that a positive **124** attitude will remove disease.

No doubt this power of analogy to produce conviction is the reason why at the time of elections, abstract thinking is very largely replaced by picturesque metaphors and analogies. Winds of change, winters of discontent, opponents trimming their sails or being left high and dry, replace the more prosaic ways of thinking in normal times. No doubt it all aids impassioned conviction, although it may be doubted whether this kind of thinking does much towards solving the real problems of the country.

Thus a Conservative speaker in the 1920s reproached a Liberal leader with 'sailing as near to the Socialist wind as he can without upsetting his frail craft.' This reference contains no grounds beyond mere assertion for the suggestion that it was the policy of the Liberals to be as left-wing as possible, but this assertion, being thrown into the form of a metaphor implying an analogy, is likely to carry more conviction than the bare verbal statement. The picture of the Liberal leader timorously edging his boat as close to the wind as he dares sticks in the mind persistently and is accepted readily; if the speaker had said bluntly what he meant instead of putting it in the form of an analogy, it is probable that his hearers would have been less inclined to believe him.

To object that sailing too near the wind is not liable to upset the boat, but only make it stop, would be to lay oneself open to a just charge of 'diversion by irrelevant objection' (Chapter 7). It shows, however, ignorance and incompetence to make such a slip in an analogy or in a metaphor for, even if the objection is not made, it will occur to the minds of many hearers and interfere with the process of creating belief. Many parliamentary candidates in coastal constituencies have aroused mirth instead of conviction by inept metaphors of fishing and sailing. Of the same order of error is the 'mixed metaphor' in which different parts of the picture suggested are inconsistent with each other, such as a newspaper report during the First World War that referred to British soldiers 'opposed to a numerical superiority of the cream of the German Army tuned to concert pitch.'

The tendency of a vivid metaphor or analogy to create conviction in the absence of rational grounds for that conviction makes possible a more extreme form of the crooked argument, which we may call the *argument from forced analogy*. In this more extreme case, the 125 argument is put into the form of an analogy or metaphor when there is insufficient resemblance between the things compared to form even a basis for expectation that they would resemble each other in the respect under discussion. A Victorian bishop said, for example, that virtue grows when watered by war's red rain. Judged rationally, this is nonsense, however effective it may have been in convincing its audience that virtue was promoted by war. The bishop might as well have said that vice grows when watered by war's red rain, or that virtue withered when sprayed by war's red defoliant. Such an argument has so little logical justification that one must attribute its use to a recognition (perhaps unconscious) of the psychological fact that analogies tend to induce belief.

The argument from forced analogy differs only in degree from the argument from mere analogy, but it is convenient to treat them as two kinds of crooked thinking since they are likely to occur in different situations, and they require different methods of refutation. Arguments from mere analogy commonly occur in serious discussions and are best dealt with by the method already employed of considering where the analogy breaks down. Forced analogies, on the other hand, are commonly found in public speeches. Their looseness is too obvious to stand against the kind of criticism they would meet in free discussion. They rely for their effect on the readiness of the mind to accept immediately any vivid metaphorical or analogical presentation of a matter. When one finds oneself driven to belief by a well-worded analogy like that of virtue watered by war's red rain, one can begin by examining how close the analogy is. Realizing that it is not at all close, one can try other analogies, as that of vice watered by war's red rain. Finding that these have no less force than the original analogy, the nature of the device used is apparent and its effect in forcing conviction disappears.

13

Oratory and suggestion

I N HIS BOOK *The Man who Mistook his Wife for a Hat* the neurophysiologist Oliver Sacks described the response of some of his brain-damaged patients to a speech by a recent American President: 'There he was … with his practised rhetoric, his histrionics, his emotional appeal – and all the patients were convulsed with laughter.'

These patients suffered from a condition known as aphasia. Damage to those parts of the brain which control speech recognition meant that they could not understand the meanings of individual words, yet they could often understand a great deal of what was said. This is because human speech does not consist of words alone; much of its meaning comes from the manner in which they are said. Aphasiacs can still appreciate some of the meaning in speech in this manner, though the understanding of the words themselves has been destroyed. Their appreciation is not just preserved; it may be enhanced, just as the hearing of blind people is often highly developed.

Thus, although the patients could not understand a word of what was being said, their highly developed sense of 'tone' made it obvious that the President was just acting. 'It was the grimaces, the histrionisms, the false gestures and, above all, the false tones and cadences of the voice, which rang false for these wordless but immensely sensitive patients. It was to these most glaring, even grotesque incongruities and improprieties that my aphasiac patients responded, undeceived and undeceivable by words.'

Another patient of Sacks's listened to the speech stony-faced. She suffered from exactly the opposite condition to aphasia, tonal agnosia. While she had no difficulty in understanding the literal meaning of the words, she could not distinguish any expression in the voice. The speech did not move her because no speech could now move her. 'He is not cogent,' she said. 'He does not speak good prose. His word use is improper. Either he is brain-damaged, or he has something to conceal.' The paradox of the President's speech was that those with intact brains were fooled into believing that the President was speaking sense and, moreover, speaking it from the heart; it was only those brain-damaged patients who were unable to respond to the combination of deceptive word use and deceptive tone who could remain undeceived. This chapter is concerned with ways in which public speakers can convince their listeners by the tone, rather than the content, of their speech.

Some of the methods used by public speakers to convince their listeners of the truth of what they say are similar to those used to hypnotize people. When a hypnotist fixes his patient with a steady gaze and in a firm, confident manner tells them that they are falling asleep, he may be able to induce the trance-like *hypnotic state*. We sometimes read that powerfully persuasive orators 'hypnotize their audiences' into believing what is required of them. That, of course, can never be literally true. The hypnotic trance is a condition startlingly different from the alert state of everyday life, and an audience that was literally hypnotized would be very unresponsive. Such an expression must only be understood as the same kind of inexact metaphor as when we speak of another audience being 'intoxicated with enthusiasm'; its members do not actually roll off their seats as if they were dead drunk. So it is better to describe these oratorical devices using the more exact technical, psychological term *tricks of suggestion*.

The psychological fact of suggestion is that if statements are made again and again in a confident manner, without argument or proof, then their hearers will tend to believe them quite independently of their soundness and of the presence or absence of evidence for their truth. The suggestions of a speaker are more likely to be accepted if they have what we may call 'prestige' – that aura that surrounds the stars of soap operas, as well as cabinet ministers, football coaches, Olympic medal winners, members of the Royal Family and other famous people.

A speaker successfully using suggestion relies, then, on three things: (1) repeated affirmation, (2) a confident, insistent method of speaking, and (3) prestige.

First, let us be clear as to what we mean by 'repeated affirmation'. We may contrast two ways of trying to make somebody else agree with us. One is to put forward the reasons we have for our belief. If we do this, we must be prepared also to consider the other person's reasons for disagreeing with us and to weigh against each other the worth of his reasons and of our own. Obviously this is a laborious method, and one that is not likely to lead to a feeling of absolute certainty on the matter in dispute. It does have the advantage that it is the one method that may help both people arguing to move towards the truth.

Such an advantage will not weigh heavily in favour of this method in the minds of those who wish for quick results – who prefer that people should act blindly and enthusiastically under their guidance rather than that they should decide calmly and wisely. For these, another method is open – that of simply saying the thing which is to be believed over and over again. This is 'repeated affirmation'.

No one could have told from first principles that mere repetition of a statement would make the hearers tend to believe that statement. That is a fact which had to be discovered – the fact that may be described by the phrase 'human suggestibility'. However, the technique is used by those wishing to influence opinion even when they have never heard the words 'suggestion' and 'suggestibility'.

During elections people's windows, blank walls, lamp-posts and even trees are covered with innumerable coloured notices simply saying 'VOTE FOR SMITH' or 'VOTE JONES, CONSERVATIVE'. These notices are clearly intended to increase the tendency of electors to vote for the named candidate. However, they do not give any reason for supposing that one would be a better member of parliament than another. If they do increase people's tendency to vote for the candidate, they do so by relying on suggestion alone. **129**

This principle is, of course, well known to advertising agencies. A rather small proportion of advertisements actually present factual information about the product in question. Most rely on some form of suggestion. The basic principle is to bring the name of the product to the attention of the consumers, preferably in the most obvious way possible. If it can be written on the side of an airship or hot-air balloon, or printed on the sides of every bus, so much the better. The psychology of advertising is a very sophisticated business – rather more so than that of political speeches, since it combines verbal and visual forms of suggestion.

The suggestion in political posters acts more powerfully if it is made also by means of speech and not merely in print, so Smith himself tours his constituency and makes speeches in which he says: 'I shall win' and 'Victory of the X party will ensure that the country is well governed.' His speech would be monotonous if he merely said these things over and over again in the same words, so he says them over and over again in different words. 'The country will be led to prosperity by our honoured and trusted leader, John Brown'; 'The British people will never support the uncaring Y party or the lunatic ideology of the Z party'; 'Our country needs a government which truly represents the people.' These phrases are worded quite differently, but they contain nothing but the two simple ideas with which we started – 'I shall win' and 'Victory of the X party will ensure that the country is well governed.'

The orator is using the method of repetition, although repeated in different words partly to avoid monotony and partly to conceal the method actually used. A speech of this kind is like a piece of music made up of one or two short tunes that occur again and again with slight variations. I once analysed part of a sermon constructed on this principle, and found that the preacher had in quite different forms repeated a single idea 31 times in the course of 13 sentences.

An example is a public speech by the British Prime Minister, Edward Heath, who was reported to have said: 'Your government, Mr Chairman, will not fail; we will succeed. The people will not lose; the people will win. The nation will not be dragged down; the nation will emerge triumphant.'

This is using the same technique as the preacher, that of repetition with variation. There are three variations of the theme 'We shall succeed', each stated once negatively and once positively. It is true that this only gives six repetitions in all, but this is only an extract from the speech; there may have been a larger number of repetitions in the whole speech.

No doubt this was effective if it was well delivered; its hearers were probably left with the conviction that the government was going to succeed. It has, however, the weakness of any purely irrational method of appeal, that the same basic material might be delivered equally effectively in the opposite sense by a speaker of the other side: 'The Conservative government, Mr Chairman, will not succeed; it will fail. The people will not win; the people will lose. The nation will not emerge triumphant; the nation will be dragged down.'

If this were equally forcibly delivered by a speaker of equal standing, this would be likely to be as persuasive as in the first form. Neither would have much effect if it were delivered to an audience sufficiently aware of the devices of crooked communication to recognize either speech as an exercise in repeated affirmation.

But the speaker does not rely merely on repetition; particular kinds of repetition are more effective than others, and other patterns of speech also help in grasping an audience's attention. Max Atkinson described in his book *Our Master's Voices* what kinds of speaking generate applause during the course of speeches. Measuring applause is a good way of finding out what gets the attention of an audience because it is evidence that people have taken in, and approved of, what the speaker has just said.

Applause is a group activity; no one wants to be the only person in the audience who is clapping. Initially applause is hesitant until the people are certain that they will be joined by a sufficiently large proportion of the audience for it to be sustained. At the Nuremberg rallies the Nazis took advantage of this by using loudspeakers to relay the audience's own applause back to themselves. Unscrupulous speakers who like to ensure that they get applause at the right moment in their speeches may prime their supporters. Provided that the bulk of the audience does not particularly object to what is being said, they are likely to follow a determined core of clappers, and to remember what the speaker just said, even if they would not have clapped without the encouragement of other members of the audience.

Even without these particularly dishonest methods, any practised speaker will have a variety of suitable techniques up their sleeve for ensuring that their audience claps. Regardless of what they are saying, they will not get sustained applause unless the audience knows exactly when to start clapping. So effective political speeches consist of distinct segments building up towards punchlines. Atkinson found that the most common pattern in this build-up was a mixture of 'three-part lists' and 'contrasts'. The extract of the speech by Edward Heath that was quoted before is a good example: each sentence is a contrast, and there are three sentences. Contrasts are perhaps effective because the first part poses a conundrum, which is resolved by the second part, effectively forming a punchline. Many other famous speeches fit this pattern. Well-known examples of contrasts and three-part lists come respectively from President Kennedy's inaugural speech – 'Ask not what your country can do for you, ask what you can do for your country' – and President Lincoln's Gettysburg address – 'Government of the people, by the people, for the people.' George Orwell's political slogan from his novel 1984 incorporates both devices – 'War is Peace; Freedom is Slavery; Ignorance is Strength.'

An audience can also be shown when to applaud by appropriate intonation and gesture. Intermediate phrases are often finished by an upward intonation, and the final one by a falling tone. Arm movements may well rise to a climax as the moment for applause approaches.

With television, these techniques have become more important than ever. It is seldom that an entire speech, or even a long extract from one, is presented. Thus in order to give the watching millions the impression of a successful speech, what is needed is a quick and quotable snippet, known as a 'sound bite', followed by a massive burst of applause (a standing ovation is a considerable bonus). The rest of the speech is of minor importance, since only the small proportion of the audience that is physically present will hear it.

The manner of delivery is also important. A half-hearted, hesitating kind of delivery has little suggestive effect. So the speaker develops the opposite manner of brazen confidence. Whatever doubts and hesitations and timidities he may feel are not allowed to appear in his manner. He thrusts out his chest, lifts up his head, and talks in **132** a steady, loud voice. It is rather difficult to do this while reading a speech since he will have to keep lowering his head to look down at the paper he is reading from, thus losing eye contact with the audience. He may avoid this problem by learning his speech off by heart. Alternatively, if he is sufficiently important, he may have access to a 'sincerity machine', which is a perspex screen upon which a script can be projected in such a way that it is visible to the speaker, but invisible to his audience. The speaker can read while at the same time appearing to look through the screen at his audience. Margaret Thatcher became a much more compelling public speaker after she started to use a 'sincerity machine'.

This confident manner is the second aid to success in suggestion. An inner feeling of certainty that one is right may be a valuable help in producing the manner, but is not essential to it. A practised speaker who has learned the trick of the confident manner can put it on like a mask. A political candidate will find it a greater help to success than any amount of expert knowledge on the work of government which they are proposing to undertake.

Speakers must be on their guard, however, against hostile hecklers who may know very well how to destroy a confident manner. If they can interject a question that makes the audience laugh at the speaker, or which makes him lose his temper even a little, the confident manner is difficult to maintain. Unless the speaker can put the heckler down with a joke it is difficult to win against a persistent interrupter from the floor. Appealing to the audience for sympathy may be successful, but the full force of the confident manner cannot be brought into use again.

A speaker will also rely on his prestige. As an external aid to this he will probably dress in a formal manner if it is a public occasion. Since a convention of modesty prevents him from telling us himself how important he is, he will often have someone to warm up the audience and increase his prestige by praise of him before he comes in. He may turn up late to emphasize how much more valuable time is to him than to his audience. This, however, is a trick that can easily backfire if the audience's appreciation of his prestige does not accord with his own.

Speakers who want to put something across to an audience by the use of suggestion are fortunate if their title, occupation or worldly **133** situation give them prestige. If they have none of these sources of prestige, they must either depend on their own oratorial gifts or else invent sources of prestige.

Many years ago I saw a man in an English market-place who was trying to sell patent medicines. He was introduced as a professor of physiology at a well-known Northern university and a great authority on physical training. He mounted a tub and began by telling us that he did not generally speak from a tub but from his own Rolls-Royce. In fact, he was clearly not a professor of physiology, and there was no reason for supposing that he was the owner of a Rolls-Royce, which would have implied that he was a wealthy and successful man. These were fictions designed to increase his prestige. Professors have a certain amount of prestige, and wealthy men have perhaps more.

I did not wait to see how much medicine he succeeded in selling; probably not much. His technique of prestige magnification was not good. His manner lacked self-confidence and he needed a shave. A real shave would have done more towards bolstering up his prestige than his imaginary Rolls-Royce.

Today public speeches play a minor part in swaying public opinion; television is much more important. News broadcasts will use brief extracts from speeches, but the main form of exposure to the populace comes from interviews and, to a lesser extent, speeches given directly to the camera. The tricks of suggestion that help to sway a remote audience sitting in front of their own televisions, being distracted by fractious children, boiling kettles and so on, are often very different from those used for a live audience.

It is difficult to imagine Adolf Hitler being a successful television politician, despite being one of the great masters of tricks of suggestion. He was an enormously effective public speaker, capable of influencing and controlling vast crowds. However, he worked on a large scale. Most of the people listening to him at the Nuremberg rallies were at a considerable distance from him. If people had been able to see him in close-up on their television screens, shouting and jumping up and down and waving his arms in a frenzy of rage, they might well have seen him just as a lunatic. While such overwrought techniques can be effective before mass audiences, this is not possible on television.

Often, small things count against people on television. Facial tics, nervous gestures or even too thick glasses or bad teeth may be more important than any powers of reasoning. One of the reasons for Richard Nixon's failure in the presidential contest against John F. Kennedy was said to be his tendency to sweat under the television lights, giving him a very shifty look in close-up. In this case, surface appearances were entirely accurate. An inevitable and unfortunate consequence of this dictatorship of the television is that major qualifications for public office tend to be negative. There is no point in having a brilliant thinker with a fine grasp of politics standing as your candidate if he happens to stammer or has some facial disfigurement. Of course, some things can be improved and politicians can be trained to discard their less agreeable mannerisms. Margaret Thatcher was trained to lower her voice so that she sounded less shrill, and thus seemed to be a warmer, more sensitive person.

The effect of television has not just been to make some personal attributes of public figures more apparent, it has also brought forward a new breed of politician. The most successful speakers are those who are relaxed and are seen to have an intimate relationship with their audience. Acting is important for this, since one must appear relaxed even under the close scrutiny of the camera, and one must be able to talk to it as if it were one's dearest friend. Perhaps the most striking example of a television politician was Ronald Reagan. His speeches seemed completely relaxed, almost formless, as if he were having a casual conversation with the entire nation. In fact, transcripts of his public pronouncements show that there was little in the way of a coherent argument. A sentence would start off well, but then descend into subclause after subclause until there was no possibility of emerging again. Despite the lack of logical structure, people were reassured by the use of comforting words. This is government by mood, not by ideas.

In public speeches, politicians can say almost anything they like without fear of interruption, except by the occasional heckler. In television interviews they are being called to account by an interviewer, who may well be hostile. Of course, interviewers cannot afford to be hostile very often or with too many people, because they may find that the supply of famous people wishing to speak to them dries up, and rudeness may gain sympathy for the victim.

The aim of the politician being interviewed is to ignore the questions they are being asked, and to give answers to a completely different set of questions that they have come prepared to answer. They must employ a battery of tricks of suggestion to convince the audience that they have actually answered the questions put to them. Perhaps the most important one a politician can use is to persuade the audience that he is a nice sincere man, doing his best to answer the questions, and that any interviewer who tries to pin him down is a most unpleasant character. It is useful to treat the interviewer as a friend initially, so that any later attempt by him to get straight answers is seen as a form of back-stabbing. Prestige does not work here. Just as bullying hecklers can be counter-productive, using the same techniques on interviewers can give a most unfortunate impression.

One cannot entirely blame politicians for their use of ready-prepared answers. Someone genuinely answering a question for which they were unprepared, and thinking about the issues raised, would probably give what appeared to be a rambling answer that would be difficult for the audience to follow. Any attempt to look at both sides of the case would look like indecision. It is much better for a politician to completely avoid this and come out with simple, well-prepared statements. However, doing this well is an indicator only of how good the briefing team is, not of the power of the politician's intellect or political ability.

After we have said all we can against the use of tricks of suggestion in public speaking, it remains true that some kind of suggestion is inescapable. If someone decides, in the interests of straight thinking, that he will not speak in a confident manner and never make any point more than once, he will not be a success as a speaker. His audience will be bored and are more likely to be impressed with his incompetence than with his honesty.

When we speak in public we must address our audience firmly and confidently, using the method of varied repetition and under the protection of as much of a halo of prestige as the chairman sees fit to provide us with. We should do this not to exploit our audience, but because it is the only efficient way of public speaking. Intellectual honesty therefore makes certain demands on us when speaking in public. We must never say in a public speech what we would not be prepared to maintain in private argument. We must not put forward as certain a statement which we think is only probably true. We must never use the politician's trick of crushing an honest objector by a dishonest reply with nothing but tricks of suggestion to support it.

Similarly, if we are giving an interview on television, we should not appear stony-faced, refuse to put make-up on and tell the interviewer what we really think of him. Our audience will be even less disposed to listen to what we are actually saying and will be more interested in our image than if we act in an ingratiating manner. However, we should concentrate on answering fairly the questions that are put to us, rather than on how to use the questions as springboards into our own prepared topics.

Intellectual honesty is not necessarily incompatible with public speaking, and there is no reason why those who value intellectual integrity should leave all the public speaking to be done by the tricksters and the exploiters of suggestibility. Yet the atmosphere of the public platform or the television studio is not favourable to intellectual honesty, and there is every reason why someone in these circumstances should examine their conscience carefully. The best protection, however, is an alert, critical and relatively unsuggestible audience, fully aware of the nature of tricks of suggestion and of the difference between such tricks and honest arguments.

14

Tricks of suggestion

THERE ARE OTHER dishonest ways of bolstering up one's prestige. For example, the trick of using obscure technical jargon is often a device for acquiring undeserved status. Many advertisements for dubious alternative medical remedies make use of bogus, semi-scientific terms such as 'quantum resonance' to support their claims. The device of using technical jargon (or something that sounds like technical jargon) for the purpose of mystifying one's hearers is not often employed as blatantly as this. We do, however, often hear people talking in an unnecessarily obscure way. This may sometimes be due to the speaker's incompetence in the use of words or to idleness, which leads them not to take the trouble to put simply what they want to say. It is also used deliberately by those who have discovered that many people are more easily impressed by what they cannot understand.

In trying to protect ourselves against such an abuse of language, we must bear in mind that our failure to understand does not necessarily imply that our opponent is trying to mystify us. He may be making a perfectly proper use of the technical language of his particular branch of knowledge. The use of a technical language not understandable to anyone who has not troubled to master it is a necessity in any branch of learning. It is a kind of intellectual shorthand that enables one to say in a sentence what could otherwise only be explained in many pages. When we meet obscurity in verbal discussion, the best reply is to ask one's opponent to explain more simply what he means. If he

138 cannot explain himself in simple language, even though he has the opportunity of doing so at great length, we may reasonably suspect him of not understanding what he means himself. It does not necessarily follow that he is using technical terms to create the impression of prestige; it may be only that he has not the necessary skill in the use of language to express himself simply. In either case we should not allow ourselves to be impressed by his obscurity as if this were a sign of his superior understanding.

Obscurity in reading matter is more difficult to deal with, since we cannot ask the author what he means. But in writing, as in speech, the mere fact that we do not understand is not in itself proof that the author is trying to impress us by deliberate obscurity. He may be talking good sense in a language we do not understand. Every science has its technical vocabulary, and it is no more reasonable to expect to be able to understand a book on psychology, physics or mathematics without first learning the technical languages of those sciences than it is to expect to be able to read a book written in Dutch if we have not first learned Dutch.

Yet the existence of technical languages gives an opportunity to those who want to use them for prestige effect. Books are often obscure because those who write them do not themselves think clearly, or because they think that people will be impressed by what they do not understand. On the other hand, an author may be obscure because his thoughts are so novel that they cannot be expressed easily in common language. Some great philosophers of the past, such as Immanuel Kant, have written in an obscure manner and many of their contemporaries judged, therefore, that their ideas were vague and meaningless. The verdict of history was that the critics were wrong. But on the whole it is more likely that what seems to be mere vagueness and emptiness of thought by those who have been educated to understand the legitimate obscurities of technical language is really so. The number of books that are hopelessly vague and meaningless is large; much larger than a charitable reader would wish to suppose.

Often people use technical language or jargon that belongs to a different world from their own. For example, there is an increasing tendency for government employees to refer to their work using the language of commerce. This partly serves to mystify the public, but is also designed to create a subconscious message similar to the use **139** of emotionally toned words described in Chapter 1. Thus taxpayers and hospital patients become customers, former permanent under-secretaries have become chief executives (with bonuses to match), and the spending of money from taxes is referred to as 'investment'. The main intention is to convey the impression that government has become more efficient by taking on the competitive rigour of the private sector. Of course, in reality this changed use of language is used simply to describe aspirations rather than achievements.

Many of the dishonest tricks that have been described earlier can be most easily carried through with a backing of prestige. A diversion (see Chapter 7), for example, can most easily be forced or a fallacy escape notice when a person of greater prestige is arguing against someone else with much less (let us say a professor against a student, or a member of parliament against one of his constituents). Indeed, the harmless protective device suggested against obscure language – that of confessing failure to understand and asking for explanation – may become a deadly weapon of dishonest argument in the hands of someone relying on prestige. Let us suppose, for example, that a professor is asked an awkward question by one of his students and that he prefers a cheap victory to an honest discussion. He may say: 'I am afraid, Mr Smith, that I cannot understand what you mean. You are too subtle for me.' It is clear that the impression left on the minds of an audience will be that the student must have been talking nonsense, for only thus would the professor have been unable to understand him.

Perhaps the best way to counter this trick is as follows. As in judo, instead of opposing the weight of his opponent the student should appear to give way to it, in order to overthrow him. He may say, for example: 'It must be my fault that you don't understand me. I'll try to put it in another way.' He can then explain what he means so fully and clearly that the simplest onlooker must understand that he has made his point.

Other controversial devices depending on suggestion are those in which the answer is in some way dictated by the question. Most simply, this happens when the question suggests its own answer, as 'Surely you accept that the world is getting warmer?' or 'You accept that the world is getting warmer, don't you?' If the person questioned is showing himself resistant to suggestion, this method can be reversed and a question asked that implies the opposite answer to that required; the questioner frames his question so as to appear to be trying to force the answer 'No', when he really wants his opponent to answer 'Yes'.

A variant of the same method is the well-known trick of asking a question so framed that any direct answer to it will imply an admission damaging to your case. 'Is global warming caused by human activities?' Clearly, either of the answers 'Yes' or 'No' implies the admission that global warming is taking place, which the person disputing may not be willing to admit. The same end can be attained by asking many different things as a complicated question demanding a single answer, as, for example, 'Do you admit that the enemy have murdered their prisoners, bombed defenceless towns, used nerve gas, and eaten sausages? Yes or no?' Plainly the person questioned might wish to answer 'Yes' to some of these questions, 'No' to others, and to make some qualifications to his answers to others. Either of the answers invited will land him in many admissions he does not want to make.

It is obvious that the first trick must be met by refusing to be influenced by the suggestion, and the second by dividing up the question and answering different parts separately. So obvious is this that one might wonder why such tricks are ever successful. It is because the tricks are used with an overbearing technique of suggestion. Without that they would have no force, and with it the correct reply may be almost impossibly difficult.

The remedy would seem to be that we should liberate ourselves, so far as we can, from the influence of suggestion. This is partly a matter of self-education. The more we know about the psychological nature of suggestion, the less will be its power over us in the ordinary situations of everyday life. Certainly we may not be able to escape its effects in all circumstances, even when we have a good understanding of its nature. We may, for example, be in the situation of being questioned by someone who not only has an authoritative manner but also has real authority over us (they may be able, for example, to make us lose our job or to send us to prison). Any use they make of the techniques of prestige suggestion will be made more effective by the favourable situation they enjoy. We may, however, succeed in reducing the effect **141** of such techniques by ourselves using as much of the confident manner as we judge to be safe, and by being aware of how we may be affected by suggestion.

There are, however, also situations in which the odds are more heavily weighted in favour of the questioner, particularly in those countries where the authorities are unrestrained by legal limits to their powers. In such situations, the questioner is not merely given authority by prestige; he may also have the power to keep the questioned person in prison, to torture them, and perhaps to end their life. The suggestibility of the person questioned may be increased by prolonged questioning, by being made to stand for many hours, by deprivation of sleep, by anxiety or by drugging. We may well doubt whether mere psychological understanding of the process would enable one in the end to resist its effects even though such understanding might be helpful in the early stages.

Some people are, however, more resistant to such situations than others. The accounts given by the more resistant suggest that the preservation of an attitude of emotional non-involvement is an important element in resistance. By emotional non-involvement is meant not responding to the questioner's anger with anger, or to their kindness with gratitude. Some have reported that they can maintain this emotional non-involvement by persisting in an attitude of contempt for their questioners; some by the harder but perhaps more effective device of persisting in an attitude of love towards them.

In Chapter 13 the question of prestige suggestion based on false credentials was raised. However, it may have legitimate foundations and yet be harmful. Titles, offices of distinction, and university degrees are all authentic props to prestige but they can all be abused. One who has mastered a subject can claim a certain amount of reasonable authority in it. If a distinguished physicist expresses an opinion on a controversial topic in physics, we may reasonably accept this opinion on their authority although we are not able ourselves to follow the reasoning that led to it. We can do this, not only because the speaker is in an academic position that implies a special knowledge of the topic under discussion, but also because there are other physicists who can follow their reasoning and check whether they are right or **142** wrong. If, however, our distinguished physicist gives an opinion on nuclear disarmament or the state of the world economy, we should give such opinions only the respectful consideration we would give to those of any other intelligent person in possession of the same facts. We should certainly not quote such pronouncements as authoritative.

Let us call an argument based on the kind of authoritative statement that depends merely on the prestige of the speaker an *appeal to mere authority*, contrasting it with an appeal to reasonable authority. There was a time when the commonest argument in intellectual dispute was the appeal to mere authority, and it was considered sufficient to support a statement by saying, 'Aristotle said so-and-so', without considering whether Aristotle had a better reason for saying what he did than we have for saying the opposite. Still, some of us are content to settle a disputed question by appealing in exactly the same way to the authority of politicians, church leaders, or even of the latest expert we have heard on television.

At one time the commonest appeal to mere authority was an appeal to the opinion of the past. 'So-and-so has always been believed' was considered to be sufficient proof that the statement in question was true. Now we are more inclined to place authority in the opinions of the present and to regard 'So-and-so is generally believed these days' as sufficient reason for accepting it as true. In all such cases we should not be hoodwinked by mere authority, but ask in the first case whether, in this particular matter, our ancestors had sound reasons for their opinion, and in the second case whether we are in this matter likely to be better informed than our parents and therefore more likely to be right. It is obvious that the modern person is more likely to be right in his opinion on such questions as the causes of infectious diseases and the nature of the stars, since many new facts have been discovered in these fields. It is not so obvious that we are in a better position than our ancestors to come to correct conclusions on questions of religion and morals. Yet it is on such questions that individuals are particularly liable to be quoted as an authority.

Personal experience can also act as a kind of prestige suggestion. An Israeli may defend aggressive policies towards the Palestinians on the grounds that he lost members of his family in the Holocaust and is prepared to take any measures to ensure that the survival of the Jewish people is never again under such a threat. Our immediate reaction is likely to be one of sympathy and we may feel inclined to accept the argument out of respect for someone who has suffered in a way that we must be thankful to have avoided.

However, this reaction is not necessarily justified. The issue under dispute is not whether the Nazis' planned extermination of the Jews was a terrible thing, since all reasonable people agree that it was one of the greatest tragedies of the last century and should never be allowed to happen again. The dispute is more likely to be about whether the particular Israeli policy under consideration is morally justified. Someone with the same personal experience could argue in the opposite way; having suffered as a member of a dispossessed race he might feel particularly sympathetic towards the Palestinians.

Similarly someone whose child has suffered brain damage soon after receiving the whooping cough vaccine may well argue persuasively against vaccinations, and will perhaps sway us in our views. But however affecting this argument is and however much it may capture our sympathy it is no more than a special case of proof by selected instances (see Chapter 6). Although subjective feelings have some part in this argument, the main issue is dependent on objective figures on the relative chances of a child suffering either from whooping cough or from being vaccinated.

Personal experience may be important in an argument that is chiefly concerned with subjective feelings. For instance, we are more likely to listen with respect to a pacifist who has been a soldier and seen the horrors of the battlefield than to an opponent who has never heard a gun fired in anger. But even in such cases we must beware of becoming uncritical of people's opinions simply out of respect for their experience.

The prestige of professors and learned men has been used to oppose many movements of scientific discovery at their beginning. The authoritative voice of the learned world put off the acceptance of Harvey's discovery of the circulation of the blood for a whole generation. Lister's life-saving discovery of the use of antiseptics in surgery was similarly opposed by medical authority when it was first made.

One must, of course, bear in mind that authority has something to be said on its side. Not all novel ideas turn out to be of value; the **144** innovator often turns out to be going down a blind alley. So it is not unreasonable for those with experience in some branch of learning to say: 'We have seen what looked like bright new ideas turning out to be mistakes. This new suggestion is one which our experience of the subject leads us to expect to be a fruitless one.' Often they will be right; occasionally they will be disastrously mistaken. In any case, it is a reason not for rejecting a new idea but for taking a cautious attitude at the beginning and subjecting it to rigorous testing before it is accepted as true. But where the prestige of authority has been used in an attempt to stifle new ideas, it has not been on any such reasonable grounds as this. Rather the authorities have said in effect: 'As authorities on this subject, we know, without any detailed examination, that this is absurd.'

Prestige suggestion has lost much of its force, and the pronouncements of 'authorities' meet with more critical intelligence and less humble acceptance than was once the case. I have heard a professor deplore the fact that modern students no longer revere their professors. God forbid that they should! It is part of the business of a professor to see that his students remain in a condition of critical alertness towards what he tells them instead of falling into this reverence, which is the emotion accompanying the acceptance of prestige suggestion. The best teachers are not those who use their prestige to force meek acceptance of what they say, but those who retain to the end of their days the spirit of students, always ready to learn more, and expecting, from those whom they have to teach, argument, contradiction, and above all, the impartial testing of the truth by experiment.

15

Straight thinking

So far we have been considering crooked thinking and dishonest arguments. This leads to the question of what kind of thinking is valid and leads to the development of genuine new ideas, and of how communication can be used for the purpose of enlightenment rather than of persuasion. Our knowledge of the dishonest tricks of argument should not lead us to suppose that there is no profitable form of discussion; the purpose of charting the rocks is to know where the deep water lies, and knowledge of the dishonest methods of argument should help us to argue in a constructive manner.

Nothing is a greater help to straightening our own thought than discussion with other people. But that discussion must be by methods very different from those of the person who sets out to convince his opponent by fair means or foul, or of the debater who regards discussion as a kind of warfare in which the aim is victory over an opponent rather than the clearing of one's own mind as well as his.

One obvious condition that must be fulfilled before a real discussion can take place is that both parties must have a sufficiently lowly opinion of the finality of their own judgements to be willing to have their opinions changed by what the other person tells them. That is a condition which many people find rather difficult to attain but, for those who do attain it, discussion with another person can result in a reasonably based change of opinion in one of two ways. First, his opponent may inform him of facts that he did not know before. Second, his opponent may point out inconsistencies between various opinions that he already holds.

opinions that he already holds.

A good example of opinions being modified by the kind of discussion in which those disputing are led to face the inconsistency between their opinions is provided by the dialogues of Socrates, as reported by Plato. In these, the method of Socrates was to ask questions of the other person, very often getting him at first to pronounce a general opinion, and then getting him to say what he thought on particular points arising from that general opinion. It then appeared that the person questioned did not agree with some of the implications of the general opinion he had first expressed, and so he was invited to revise that general opinion until he had stated it in a way which led to no conclusion that he would not accept. For example, in the opening pages of *The Republic*, one of the companions of Socrates put forward an opinion on the nature of justice as 'giving every man what is due to him'. By questioning the man who put forward this view, Socrates managed to convince him that this way of looking at justice implied other things which the man did not believe to be true, such as that justice was only useful to those who are at war, or only useful for things that are not used, and also that the just man was a sort of thief. Since these seemed to be implied by the view that justice was giving every man his due, and since the man who had said that justice was giving every man his due did not believe these implications of his opinion about justice, he was led to conclude that he did not really believe that justice was giving every man his due.

He had thus been led to change his opinion as a result of discussion, by having been shown that his opinion implied something that he thought was not true. Discussion was of value to him in straightening out his thought by revealing inconsistencies that he had not suspected. This is an example of how discussion may help straight thinking when the discussion is honest, and the people discussing are willing to change their minds. Indeed, an objection one can have to the Socratic dialogues as examples of straight discussion is that Plato makes it always appear that it was those who argued with Socrates who were led to change their minds, while Socrates himself never seemed to do so.

It might be supposed that all that Socrates was doing might as well have been done by his companions themselves. He was revealing inconsistencies that were already present in their own thought; in other words, he was showing them what they really thought. If he was just doing that, it looks as if they might as well have done it for themselves. In a sense they might, but probably would not have done. We can all have many inconsistent opinions whose inconsistency we are not able to recognize until someone else shows it to us. I was once doing an experiment on a group of people to find the degree of self-consistency of their opinions. The amount of inconsistency revealed in their answers was surprising. For example, a large number both asserted that every statement in the Bible was literally true, and denied that Jonah emerged alive after having been swallowed by a great fish. It was not that they did not know that the Bible stated that Jonah was swallowed by a great fish and afterwards came out alive; it was merely that these were two opinions which they had formed separately without relating them to one another. It is unlikely that they would have been brought into relationship by the person's own thinking since the realization of the lack of consistency in one's own thought is a somewhat uncomfortable experience that the mind tries to avoid.

Such communication or thinking, producing rationally grounded changes in opinion, may be called 'productive'. That an argument in the form of a syllogism (see Chapter 8) can be genuinely productive is often hidden from students of logic by the trivial and absurd example of a typical syllogism that the textbooks of logic have inherited from Aristotle:

> All men are mortal,
> Socrates is a man,
> Therefore, Socrates is mortal.

Aristotle was a great thinker, so one may charitably suppose that he made up this ridiculous example of an argument on the spur of the moment, thinking that he could substitute a better one tomorrow, and happily not realizing that this would be preserved to confuse students of logic for 2,000 years. It is plainly non-productive; no one has ever said after he heard it: 'I see. Socrates will die too. I never realized that before.' No new information is generated by this pseudo-argument because no one could know that all men were mortal unless

they already knew that Socrates was mortal.

There can, however, be thinking of the same general pattern that does really generate new knowledge. For instance, suppose that I am going to vote in an election. There are four voting rooms and I do not know which of these I am supposed to use. I ask an official and he asks me my name. When I have told him, he says: 'Those whose names begin with T vote in room 3.'

What has happened may be expressed in the form of a syllogism:

> Those whose names begin with T vote in room 3.
> Thouless has a name beginning with T,
> Therefore, Thouless votes in room 3.

Unlike the Socrates argument, this does really generate a new piece of knowledge. The conclusion was not previously known either to the official or to myself. He knew the first premise; I knew the second. It was only when these two came together that the conclusion emerged. This is a very elementary form of productive thinking. More typically, the form of a productive argument is that in which a general principle is put forward as the first premise. This may be agreed to by both disputants. One of the disputants then puts forward a particular case of that general principle that leads to a conclusion that is unacceptable to the other.

Let us suppose, for example, that X is defending a pacifist position which Y does not accept. Neither X nor Y approves of murder and X has no difficulty in getting Y to accept the general principle that it is wrong to destroy human life. X makes this the first premise of his argument. It differs from the first premise in the Socrates argument in the fact that we all assent to general moral principles without considering all the particular cases to which they can be applied. Y may, for example, assent to the proposition that it is wrong to destroy human life because he finds the idea of taking life repulsive or because he accepts the authority of the Sixth Commandment, 'Thou shalt not kill.' X makes a new application of this agreed principle when he points out to Y that making war destroys human life, a statement that cannot be reasonably denied by Y. X then concludes that it is wrong to make war, which is a proposition previously denied by Y, but which he must admit necessarily follows from premises that he has agreed to.

X's argument may be put in the form:

> All destroying of human life is wrong,
> War is a destroying of human life,
> Therefore, war is wrong.

This is a productive argument of sound logical form, and its rational upshot for Y must be one of two things. First, he may change his mind about the conclusion, and now agree that war is wrong, perhaps saying that he never thought of the matter in that way before. Alternatively (and more probably) he will modify his acceptance of the first premise and say that he does not really accept the proposition that all destroying of human life is wrong, but only the destroying of life under certain specified conditions, such as for one's private gain or for revenge, but that it is right when ordered by lawful authorities as in executions or in war. In either case, something has been accomplished by the argument; Y's opinions have been changed by it.

Most arguments do not end with one of the disputants admitting that he has been in error or even with both parties changing their opinions, but an argument can be productive even if both sides go away convinced that they were in the right all along. It may have been productive because the people involved came to a better understanding of the nature of their disagreement. If the arguments of both sides are logical, with their conclusions following strictly from their premises, and neither side makes a factual error or misuses a word, then they may still have differences resulting from different fundamental assumptions about the world. Discovering exactly what these differences are may make them more tolerant of each other's opinions, or at least stop them trying to persuade the other of the rational superiority of their own case.

It is probably this form of productive argument that is the most important in practical affairs. It is only once you have a clear idea of the differences that separate you from your opponent that true compromise can be sought successfully. However unpopular that idea of compromise may be to the modern world, distrustful of the half-solutions and uncertainties of liberalism, it remains true that the only true resolution of differences between two parties must involve some kind of compromise.

16

The future of straight thinking

THE FIRST EDITION of this book, published in 1930, ended with a plea for the application of the scientific attitude of dispassionate reasonableness to national and international affairs. The establishment of the League of Nations was a small beginning in the task of moderating the blind and uncontrolled forces of rivalry between nations. What was needed in addition was a well-educated population, distrustful of emotional phraseology and all the rest of the stock-in-trade of the exploiters of crooked thinking, and devoid of excessive reverence for ancient institutions and ancient ways of thinking, which could take conscious control of our social development and could destroy those plagues of our civilization – war, poverty and crime.

Today these words seem unduly optimistic in view of the events that followed soon after: the realization that the League of Nations was completely powerless, the rise of Adolf Hitler on a wave of emotionally charged propaganda, the coming of the Second World War and its replacement by the Cold War. Things have not improved greatly since then. The United Nations, successor to the League of Nations, has gained little more influence; even in the most advanced Western nations, irrational forces are powerful and people are following paths of folly. Unnecessary wars are being fought, people are destroying their own livelihood and hope for the future by environmental damage and uncontrolled population growth.

The ideal of dispassionate scientific reasonableness has not only failed to become generally accepted for dealing with controversial matters, but has been rejected by many people. The scientific approach is seen not as a saviour but as one of the causes of our present problems. There are several reasons for this. One is the confusion between science and technology, the latter being the practical application of scientific advances. The unthinking use of technology has undoubtedly caused many problems, but this is an argument in favour of considering the dangers as well as the benefits of technological advances, rather than an argument against science.

There are also objections to science itself. They come from people who dislike the experimental methods employed, or are concerned about socially undesirable results which might emerge from a set of experiments or observations. The first can be a perfectly valid objection; the second most certainly is not. The chief exponents of political control of the direction of science were Stalin and Hitler, and their precedent is not one that modern politicians should be too keen to follow. However uncomfortable a particular truth may be to live with, it is always better to face up to it than to pretend that it is not there.

The erosion of public confidence in science and the scientific way of thinking has been exacerbated by a change in the way that scientists view the history of their subject. In the first half of the last century the development of science was presented as a single path leading ever onwards and upwards, with every generation refining and purifying the truth. Such a simplistic view failed to take account of all the blind alleys. Also, theories are not suddenly overturned by brilliant experiments, but remain generally accepted, despite evidence to the contrary, until social conditions become favourable to new theories. This modern view has been overstated in the idea that science has no genuine claim to objective truth, but is merely a reflection of contemporary culture. It still remains true that despite all the red herrings and areas of stagnation, the general direction of science has been towards a greater refining of the truth.

Much more worrying than any cynicism in people's attitudes towards scientific objectivity is the resurgence of dogmatic belief systems. Perhaps at this point we should make it clear what we mean by a dogmatic belief system and how it differs from any other kind of belief system.

We all believe in the truth of things that cannot be directly observed. Some of these are internal sensations like hunger or love, which are common to all people. Other beliefs differ between people and between cultures. Many are concerned with how one ought to behave – with ethical issues of right and wrong. With the exception of a few psychopaths, we all hold a set of such beliefs and indeed it would be difficult to make decisions about one's life without them. People hold these beliefs with differing levels of conviction. Some people's ideas of right and wrong are passively absorbed from their own culture, and after visiting another country such people may realize that a completely different set of beliefs could be just as good. On the other hand, many truly believe that their beliefs are right in an absolute sense. In either case, if the beliefs form a coherent set, adhered to by a large number of people, they are likely to be called a religion. There is a great deal of opportunity within religious thought and beliefs for the exercise of crooked thinking and for the kind of thinking that prevents the solution of the world's most serious problems.

The existence of other people with completely different sets of equally strongly held beliefs to one's own presents problems that were discussed in more general terms in Chapter 9. There are two ways of dealing with these problems. One is to accept that one's own beliefs are not necessarily the only valid ones, and that truth can appear in many forms. A more cynical form of this approach is to say that even if one believes other people to be deluded, telling them so may not be the best way of coming to any agreement on practical matters. The other approach is to say that one's own system of belief is the only true one and that other people are simply wrong. It is this view that is such an obstacle to progress, and prevents any possibility of productive dialogue. In the past people held this kind of dogmatic belief with more excuse – they had little contact with other sorts of people. Today no such excuse is possible.

Apart from the difficulty of coming to terms with people holding different views, there are other problems caused by adherence to a dogmatic set of beliefs. They tend to present the world as a simple place and to lead people to the illusion that real problems have simple solutions. It is clear that the world is not simple and to interpret it as such requires much to be overlooked or ignored.

Another difficulty with dogmatic beliefs is that they come on an all-or-nothing basis. In most cases they do not deal just with moral imperatives but also with the nature of facts, in ways that can be disproved, at least in theory. If a part of a belief system is disproved, its adherents have the choice of rejecting the whole or turning a blind eye to the contradiction, and re-describing reality to conform to the dogma. Perhaps the most striking examples of this come from Marxism, the ideology that dominated much political thinking during the time when the first four editions of this book were written.

The basis of Marxism is a theory about the development of human societies. Karl Marx's study of history suggested to him that societies went through several stages of development. Primitive societies turned into feudal ones, which evolved into capitalist societies. In these the ruling classes, the bourgeoisie, did not own the workers, the proletariat, but paid for their labour. As a result of the inherent conflicts within such a society and the impoverishment of the proletariat under capitalism, Marx predicted that revolution would follow. The resulting 'dictatorship of the proletariat' would develop into fully fledged communism, in which the class system would finally have been destroyed and mankind would live in brotherhood and bliss.

This is a very useful theory. It gave the world an important new way of looking at history and the economic forces shaping societies. However, Marxism went beyond the status of a political theory. Its central tenets, including the importance of class struggle, the inevitability of the victory of the proletariat in the class war and the superiority of a planned economy over free enterprise, became articles of faith in a religion. Marxism lays itself open to testing rather more than most religions, since it makes specific predictions about how history will progress.

It is more than 100 years since Marx formulated his theory and there has been plenty of opportunity to test it against the reality of history. It simply failed the test of time. Capitalist societies have proved much more resistant than Marx expected, and the countries that experienced revolutions, notably Russia and China, were feudal rather than capitalist when they occurred. There are now very few Marxist states left. However, in those countries in which it is given the status of a religion the theory cannot be rejected because it would mean abandoning too much. If there is a problem in reconciling Marxist theory with reality, then the words used to describe reality are redefined. The result is that words and reality are completely dissociated.

This doctrinaire approach to reality, shown not only by Marxists but also fundamentalist Christians, Muslims and many other groups, is probably the single most important obstacle to straight thinking in the world today. What is needed instead of reliance on a book or set of doctrines as the one and only source of truth is the realization that we are bound by a common humanity, and that realization should be the basis of any system of belief.

There have been many other changes in the way that language is used and misused since the first edition of this book was published. Some of these have been discussed in previous chapters, such as the decrease in respect for prestige arguments, the greater tolerance to being 'shocked', the changes in style of public speaking that come from the importance of television, and so on.

Perhaps one of the most important changes is the reduced impact of words compared with pictures. It is easy to overstate the importance of this change if one lives in those parts of the world where television is paramount, but it is a major change nevertheless. While a picture may be worth a thousand words, it is much easier to analyse the thousand words and discover whether they are truthful or lying than to discover whether a picture is lying or not. A single photograph or some film footage may accurately record what is before the camera, but the scene that is observed may be unrepresentative of what is actually going on. This is a visual example of 'proof by selected instance' but may be much more difficult to pin down than the verbal form.

A major advantage of the increased importance of pictures in our lives is that other people's lives are brought immediately to our attention. We have much more idea of the reality of what it is like to be a Sudanese peasant or Chinese factory worker than was possible before, and it is impossible to deny our shared humanity. This exposure to what the rest of the world is like makes prejudice a much less natural feeling. The disadvantage is that we can become overwhelmed by **155** seeing the misery and the problems that the world is facing so clearly laid out. Individuals may feel that their own contribution would make an incredibly small difference, and so turn their backs on the real and dull problems that face the world like infant malnutrition, sewage disposal and soil erosion. Only exceptional emergencies like droughts and floods can persuade people to turn out their pockets. If people's attitudes to the poorer parts of the world were determined by words – explanations of the underlying economic causes of poverty – rather than by pictures that produce an emotional reaction to extreme suffering, our responses to such problems might be more sustained and more rational.

Another major change in the use of language that has occurred in the last 50 years is the reluctance to use the language of prejudice. In the works of Rudyard Kipling we come across phrases such as 'half devil half child', used to describe people under colonial rule. While we may be able to read much of Kipling's writings today with admiration for his mastery of prose and his humanity, phrases like these are embarrassing to us. However, the use of language may have changed much more than people's attitudes. The prejudices that were expressed openly in the past may be concealed beneath language dealing with cultural differences. While this use of language may be hypocritical it has the advantage that prejudice seems unnatural, and as people grow up with this feeling, prejudice itself as well as its language may die out. In the same way, one may approve of the lip service paid to human rights and the equality of mankind even in those countries where human rights are most conspicuously lacking. The attempt to redefine 'democratic' as in 'Democratic People's Republic of Korea', or free speech as 'speech that does not criticize the state' may be unattractive, but the formal recognition that democracy and free speech are good things can be seen as a positive sign, even if their current use is callous cynicism.

On the other hand, excessive concern with the way that words are used, rather than the facts that they describe, has led to the distraction of attention away from real issues. For example, the feminist insistence on the use of gender-neutral words has meant that public
attention has focused on these symptoms of a historical attitude to

differences between sexual roles rather than on the real economic and social forces that have prevented women from gaining equality.

The improvements in the use of language and communication that were anticipated in the first edition of this book have not come about, although the precise forms that crooked thinking takes have changed. It is unfortunate that the need to point out the differences between straight and crooked thinking is still there and that this book still seems to have some value. However, its message is still as relevant as ever. If we do not use language as a tool to unite us instead of as a weapon to destroy our opponents we shall be overwhelmed by the problems that the world must deal with. Disaster stares us in the face unless we can take control of our own destiny. We cannot unite against the common enemies of environmental destruction, poverty, war and changing climate unless we learn to think straight and communicate effectively with each other.

Appendix 1:
Thirty-seven dishonest tricks commonly used in argument, with the methods of overcoming them

IN MOST TEXTBOOKS of logic there is to be found a list of 'fallacies', classified in accordance with the logical principles they violate. Such collections are interesting and important, and it is to be hoped that any readers who wish to go more deeply into the principles of logical thought will turn to these works. The present list is, however, something quite different. Its aim is practical and not theoretical. It is intended to be a list that can be conveniently used for detecting dishonest modes of thought, which we shall actually meet in arguments and speeches. Sometimes more than one of the tricks mentioned would be classified by the logician under one heading, some he would omit altogether, while others that he would include are not to be found here. Practical convenience and practical importance are the criteria I have used in this list.

If we have a plague of flies in the house we buy insecticides and not a treatise on the biology of Dipterans. This implies no sort of disrespect for zoologists, or for the value of their work as a first step in the effective control of flies. The present book bears to the treatises of logicians the relationship of insecticides to learned biological texts.

Straight & Crooked Thinking

Other books have been concerned with the appraisal of the whole of an argumentative passage without such analysis into sound and unsound parts as I have attempted. Undoubtedly it is also important to be able to say of an argued case whether it has or has not been established by the arguments brought forward. Mere detection of crooked elements in the argument is not sufficient to settle this question since a good argumentative case may be disfigured by crooked arguments. The study of crooked thinking is, however, an essential preliminary to this problem of judging the soundness of an argued case. It is only when we have cleared away the emotional thinking, the selected instances, the inappropriate analogies, etc., that we can see clearly the underlying case and make a sound judgement as to whether it is right or wrong.

The 37 dishonest tricks of argument described in this book are:

1 *The use of emotionally toned words* (Chapter 1).
Dealt with by translating the statement into emotionally neutral words.

2 *Discussing a verbal proposition as if it were a factual one, or failing to disentangle the verbal and factual elements in a proposition that is partly both* (Chapter 2).
This is really an incompetent rather than a dishonest way of arguing. The remedy is to point out how much of the question at issue is a difference in the use of words and how much (if at all) it is a difference as to fact or values.

3 *Putting forward a tautology (such as, that too much of the thing attacked is bad) as if it were a factual judgement* (Chapter 2).
Dealt with by pointing out that the statement is necessarily true from its verbal form.

4 *Change in the meaning of a term during the course of an argument* (Chapter 3).
Dealt with by getting the term defined or by substituting an equivalent form of words at one of the points where the term in question is used, and seeing whether the use of this form of words affects the truth of the statement.

5 *The use of a dilemma which ignores a continuous series of possibilities between the two extremes presented* (Chapter 4).

Dealt with by refusing to accept either alternative, but pointing to the fact of the continuity which the person using the argument has ignored. Since this is likely to appear over-subtle to an opponent using the argument, it may be strengthened by pointing out that the argument is the same as that of saying, 'Is this paper black or white?' when it is, in fact, a shade of grey.

6 *The use of the fact of continuity between them to throw doubt on a real difference between two things (the 'argument of the beard')* (Chapter 4).
Dealt with by pointing out that the difference is nevertheless real. This again may be made stronger by pointing out that application of the same method of argument would deny the difference between 'black' and 'white' or between 'hot' and 'cold'.

7 *Illegitimate use of or demand for definition* (Chapter 4).
If an opponent uses definitions to pin down facts which are not clear-cut, it is necessary to point out to him how much more complicated facts are in reality than in his words. If he tries to drive you to define for the same purpose, the remedy is to refuse formal definition but to adopt some other method of making your meaning clear.

8 *Use of a bad implied definition* (Chapter 5).
Dealt with by asking the speaker exactly how he defines the word.

9 *Making a statement in which 'all' is implied but 'some' is true* (Chapter 6).
Dealt with by putting the word 'all' into the statement and showing that it is then false.

10 *Proof by selected instances* (Chapter 6).
Dealt with dishonestly by selecting instances opposing your opponent's contention or honestly by pointing out the true form of the proof (as a statistical problem in association) and either supplying the required numerical facts or pointing out that your opponent has not got them.

11 *Extension of an opponent's proposition by contradiction or by misrepresentation of it* (Chapter 7).
Dealt with by stating again the more moderate position that is being defended.

12 *Diversion to another question, to a side issue, or by irrelevant objection* (Chapter 7).

Dealt with by refusing to be diverted from the original question, but stating again the real question at issue.

13 *Proof by inconsequent argument* (Chapter 7).

Dealt with by asking that the connection between the proposition and the alleged proof may be explained, even though the request for explanation may be attributed to ignorance or lack of logical insight on the part of the person making it.

14 *The argument that we should not make efforts against X which is admittedly evil because there is a worse evil Y against which our efforts should be directed* (Chapter 7).

Dealt with by pointing out that this is a reason for making efforts to abolish Y, but no reason for not also making efforts to get rid of X.

15 *The recommendation of a position because it is a mean between two extremes* (Chapter 7).

Dealt with by denying the usefulness of the principle as a method of discovering the truth. In practice, this can most easily be done by showing that our own view also can be represented as a mean between two extremes.

16 *Pointing out the logical correctness of the form of an argument whose premises contain doubtful or untrue statements of fact* (Chapter 8).

Dealt with by refusing to discuss the logic of the argument but pointing out the defects of its presentations of alleged fact.

17 *The use of an argument of logically unsound form* (Chapter 8).

Since the unsoundness of such arguments can be easily seen when the form of the argument is clearly displayed, an opponent who does this can be dealt with by making such a simple statement of his argument that its unsoundness is apparent. For one's own satisfaction when reading an argument of doubtful soundness, it will often be found useful to make a diagram.

18 *Argument in a circle* (Chapter 8).

19 *Begging the question* (Chapter 8).

Both 18 and 19 can be dealt with in the same way as 17; by restating our opponent's argument in such a simple way that the nature of the device used must be clear to anyone.

20 *Overcoming resistance to a doubtful proposition by a preliminary statement of a few easily accepted ones* (Chapter 9).

Knowledge of this trick and preparedness for it are the best safe-guards against its effects.

21 *Statement of a doubtful proposition in such a way that it fits in with the thought-habits or the prejudices of the hearer* (Chapters 9/10).

A habit of questioning what appears obvious is the best safe-guard against this trick. A particular device of value against it is to restate a questionable proposition in a new context in which one's thought-habits do not lead to its acceptance.

22 *Angering an opponent in order that he may argue badly* (Chapter 10).

Dealt with by refusing to get angry however annoying our opponent may be.

23 *Special pleading* (Chapter 10).

Dealt with by applying one's opponent's special arguments to other propositions that he is unwilling to admit.

24 *Commending or condemning a proposition because of its practical consequences to the hearer* (Chapter 10).

We can only become immune to the effect of this kind of appeal if we have formed a habit of recognizing our own tendencies to be guided by our prejudices and by our own self-interest, and of distrusting our judgement on questions in which we are practically concerned.

25 *Argument by attributing prejudices or motives to one's opponent* (Chapter 10).

Best dealt with by pointing out that other prejudices may equally well determine the opposite view, and that, in any case, the question of why a person holds an opinion is an entirely different question from that of whether the opinion is or is not true.

26 *The use of generally accepted formulae of predigested thought as premises in argument* (Chapter 11).

The best way of dealing with predigested thinking in argument is to point out good-humouredly and with a backing of real evidence that matters are more complicated than your opponent supposes.

27 *'There is much to be said on both sides, so no decision can be made either way', or any other formula leading to the attitude of academic detachment* (Chapter 11).

Dealt with by pointing out that taking no action has practical consequences no less real than those that result from acting on either of the propositions in dispute, and that this is no more likely than any other to be the right solution of the difficulty.

28 *Argument by mere analogy* (Chapter 12).

Dealt with by examining the alleged analogy in detail and pointing out where it breaks down.

29 *Argument by forced analogy* (Chapter 12).

The absurdity of a forced analogy can best be exposed by showing how many other analogies supporting different conclusions might have been used.

30 *Suggestion by repeated affirmation* (Chapter 13).

31 *Suggestion by use of a confident manner* (Chapter 13).

32 *Suggestion by prestige* (Chapter 13).

The best safeguard against all three of these tricks of suggestion is a theoretical knowledge of suggestion, so that their use may be detected. All three devices lose much of their effect if the audience sees how the effect is being obtained, so merely pointing out the fact that the speaker is trying to create conviction by repeated assertion in a confident manner may be enough to make this device ineffective. Ridicule is also often used to undermine the confident manner, or any kind of criticism that makes the speaker begin to grow angry or plaintive.

33 *Prestige by false credentials* (Chapter 13).

The obvious remedy for this is, when practicable, to expose the falsity of the titles, degrees, etc., that are used. The prestige then collapses.

34 *Prestige by the use of pseudo-technical jargon* (Chapter 14).

Best dealt with by asking in a modest manner that the speaker should explain himself more simply.

35 *Affectation of failure to understand backed by prestige* (Chapter 14).

Dealt with by more than ample explanation.

36 *The use of questions drawing out damaging admissions* (Chapter 14).

Dealt with by refusal to make the admissions. The difficulty of this refusal must be overcome by any device reducing one's suggestibility to the questioner.

37 *The appeal to mere authority* (Chapter 14).

Dealt with by considering whether the person supposed to have authority had a sound reason for making the assertion that is attributed to him.

Appendix 2:
A discussion illustrating crooked thinking

I N ORDER TO illustrate the foregoing list of dishonest arguments (Appendix 1) I have devised an imaginary television interview of two opposing politicians in which as many dishonest devices as possible are used. The arguments have been chosen to illustrate crooked thinking, so that the whole conversation is perhaps worse than an average sample of political debate. Most of the arguments, however, are identical with or similar in form to ones that I have heard used in real interviews. I do not think that any part of the conversation is more crooked and unsound than can be heard at any place where political discussion is carried on, although I admit that it would be difficult to find, in practice, a debate in which there is so sustained a failure to argue 'straight' on any problem. To that extent the passage is a caricature, but a caricature made up of natural fragments.

I suggest that, at a first reading, readers should cover up my notes on the debate, and write down all the pieces of crooked argumentation or thought that they can detect in the passage, referring when possible to numbers in the list of dishonest tricks in Appendix 1. Afterwards they may wish to compare the fallacies they have detected with those pointed out in my notes. My notes do not claim to be either exhaustive or unprejudiced, and many readers will no doubt make a different list that has as much claim to be considered right as my own.

Those taking part in the discussion are C, a Conservative politician, L, a Labour politician, I, the interviewer and A, members of the audience.

Straight & Crooked Thinking

I After all the talking, all the speculation and all the contradictory opinion polls we are about to find out what the people of this nation really believe when they finally get to the voting stations. L, what do you think they will decide?

L I have every confidence in the good sense of the British people.[1] At long last they will turn away from faceless[2] capitalism and return to a caring society.[3] Power must return to the people.[4] For too long it has been in the hands of the money-grubbers, the mean-spirited seekers after riches and the philistines of profit-making.[5] It must return to the people[6] who really care. Labour must return to office.

I Do you agree with this, C?

C No, it is complete and utter nonsense.[7] The British people have too much sense to be taken in by this purple prose. What they really want is a continued period of sound and sensible government,[8] with none of this woolliness and emotional rhetoric.

I Thank you. Now perhaps we can have some questions from the audience?

A I should like to ask C if he doesn't find it difficult to justify cutting income taxes for the very rich when there are so many people starving in the Third World?

---

[1] This is a sentence which has very little meaning, but by flattering the British people, presumably including the studio audience, L hopes to lead them on to accept his more controversial statements that follow it (no. 20).

[2] Faceless in this case is used only for emotional effect and could equally well be replaced by another emotional word, such as 'naked' to achieve the same effect, though with a very different literal meaning (no. 1).

[3] The implication here is that the electorate is faced with two stark possibilities, harsh capitalism or kindly socialism, with no possibility of a middle ground between them (no. 5).

[4] L could very well be accused of woolliness for using the word *people* in this way.

[5] L has repeated himself, saying essentially the same thing in three different ways, using much emotional language in the process (no. 30).

[6] L uses the word *people* again, this time referring to just the Labour Party, rather than the whole electorate (no. 4). This is not seriously misleading, but may have the effect of persuading that the Labour Party has some closer affinity with ordinary people than do its opponents.

[7] This is a popular combination of words often used by politicians. It is designed to convey complete conviction without the presentation of any facts (no. 31).

[8] *Sound and sensible* is a phrase with more emotional than factual meaning (no. 1). A government which appears 'sound and sensible' to its supporters will be called 'conventional and uninspired' by its opponents.

C As a Minister of the Crown[9] I am faced with many difficult decisions. Of course we would all like to relieve poverty and suffering everywhere we can, but things are not as simple as that. We feel that the best way to remove poverty is to increase prosperity.[10] To do that we must keep income taxes low as an incentive to the producers in our society to make money, and if they make money we shall all be richer and have so much more to give to the poor people.[11]

L That is all very well, but the fact is that a smaller proportion of total government expenditure has gone on overseas aid than ever before.

C I think what you are forgetting is that charity begins at home.[12] I am all in favour of aid and development projects in the poorer parts of the world, but there is a time when enough is enough, especially when there are hungry people at home.[13]

L Even at home the number of people living in poverty has increased. That sounds more like poverty beginning at home, not charity beginning at home.

C Well, that all depends on what you mean by poverty. Do you mean people whose declared income is below the official poverty line? Well, let me tell you that many of those people are doing very well doing unofficial jobs while they are claiming the dole.[14] Only last week in my constituency a case was found of a man who had signed on the dole for the last five years and who owns a Jaguar and five race-horses.[15] Is this what you mean by poverty?

[9] He begins by appealing to his prestige (no. 32).
[10] Although this statement is a tautology in its basic form (no. 3), there are a number of words missing in the argument. The poverty he is being asked about is abroad, while the prosperity he is talking about is in his own country.
[11] C here presents a very complicated argument in an oversimplified form (predigested argument) (no. 26).
[12] This is a very common form of predigested thought, which means nothing (no. 26).
[13] C is not proposing additional measures to relieve poverty at home, but using this as a reason for doing nothing about poverty abroad (no. 14).
[14] This is a diversion (no. 12), since he has escaped from the problem of overseas aid.
[15] This is an example of proof by selected instance (no. 10). He could equally well have mentioned the case in the same week of the man in his constituency who was reduced to selling his war medals to pay his heating bill.

L Haven't you seen all the homeless sleeping rough on our streets? That is poverty by anyone's standards.[16]

C We are doing all that we can to deal with these problems, but it is no use for the Labour Party to go on about poverty, while proposing a completely unrealistic programme of massive increases in spending without similarly huge increases in taxation.

I How do you answer that one? On one hand you are trying to increase money spent on social security and the health services, but you are not saying where all this extra money will come from.

L What worries me more is how the Conservative Party can justify cutting social security. Soon there will be people starving on the streets.[17]

I That was not exactly the question I was asking. The audience will be very interested to know if you are planning to raise income taxes to fulfil your promises.

L I was just getting round to that.[18] If we do have to raise income taxes it will be through no fault of our own but because of the shortsightedness of the Conservatives. Their cuts have caused enormous long-term damage to our health services. Everyone knows that our hospitals are an absolute disgrace because so little money is put into upkeep and maintenance.[19]

C That is nonsense, and you know it. We have put an enormous amount of money into the National Health Service,

---

[16] L makes the mistake of following the diversion, and failing to pursue the original argument. However, he successfully answers C's attempt to extract a precise definition from him (no. 7).

[17] L is put in a difficult position here. He is asked a question that he wants to avoid, so he adopts the usual policy of ignoring the real question but picking on one element (in this case social security payments) to launch a diversionary attack on his opponent (no. 12), at the same time extending his opponent's position by misrepresentation (no. 11).

[18] The interviewer has forced L back from his diversion, so in order to conceal it L pretends that he was constructing an argument that was leading towards the point at issue, and that his train of logic was interrupted by the interviewer. Apart from covering his tracks, this approach has the advantage that the interviewer will seem very aggressive if he tries to force the point again.

[19] The next diversion, again in the form of an attack on the other side, pays lip-service to the interviewer's attempts to get the original question answered, by mentioning the words 'income tax', but still avoids the issue.

but also we have inherited an obsolete and creaking bureaucracy. What the NHS needs is not more money, but a more rational and accountable management. What it needs is more efficiency, and it has been shown that market forces are the only way to achieve this.[20]

L Exactly. What you are trying to do is to abolish the NHS[21] and get us back to the days when young children[22] were dying on the streets because their parents could not afford to pay for a doctor.

C I did not say that we want to abolish the NHS. What I said is that it needs to be reformed, and people's attitudes need to be reformed too. Too much mollycoddling is a bad thing.[23] What happens now is that because treatment is free, people go to the doctor for any trivial little complaint. We are aiming to make people more self-reliant.

A Many women are concerned about the threat to their liberty posed by the proposal to reduce the time limit at which abortions are available. Don't you believe that it is a woman's right to choose what to do with her own body?[24]

L Yes of course, but I don't think that the issue is quite as simple as that. There is a more fundamental right, and that is the right to life for all human beings.[25] I know that some people say that an unborn child early in development does not matter and that abortion is acceptable up to a certain time.

---

[20] C has been forced to follow the diversion, since he is left with the choice of doing this or appearing to make a dangerous admission by not answering the attack.
[21] Again C's position has been extended (no. 11).
[22] As usual children are brought into the argument for emotional effect. Adults as well as children will suffer from costly medical treatment. It may be that the effects are worse for children, but that is not why L mentioned them. He is taking advantage of emotional habits of thought in connection with children (no. 21). In the same way an opponent of violence will be asked: 'Wouldn't you consider it right to use force to protect a helpless child who was being maltreated by a powerful and brutal man?' He is never asked the equally reasonable question: Wouldn't you consider it right to use force to protect a helpless middle-aged stockbroker who was being maltreated by a powerful and brutal man?'
[23] This is a tautology, just as 'Too much private medicine is a bad thing' is a tautology (no. 3).
[24] The questioner is begging the question, because the issue under discussion is whether a foetus can be considered part of a woman's body or has separate rights (no. 19).
[25] L is also begging the question, since his opponent would not accept that a foetus early in pregnancy could be considered as a human being.

The point is that you cannot just draw a line and say that after that time the unborn child is a living person with all its rights and the previous day it was just a lump of meat. Abortion can really only be justified if it is necessary to save the life of the mother, and even then I think that one must be really careful.

A What if the foetus[26] is going to be born terribly deformed? Would you condemn it to a life of suffering?

L It is very dangerous to talk in those terms. If you start killing unborn children then you may very soon find people recommending euthanasia or infanticide on the same grounds.[27]

I C, what do you feel about this subject? How will you be voting when the issue comes up?

C This is a very complicated issue. There are cases where abortion may be necessary for the sake of the mother, but on the other hand the sanctity of human life is a very important principle. My feeling is that some intermediate position is the reasonable one;[28] we should allow abortions under some circumstances, but make sure that there really are good reasons.

I So how will you vote on a bill to reduce the time limit for abortion?

C I don't think that reducing the time limit really gets to the heart of the problem, which is to do with the reasons why women have abortions, so I shall probably abstain on this issue.[29]

I I am afraid that is all we have time for. I want to thank the audience for their probing questions and the speakers for their candid answers to the questions that have been raised. You have given us a clear view of some of the issues on which voters will be deciding in the coming election.

---

[26] A, being in favour of abortion, uses the word 'foetus' while her opponent describes the same thing as an 'unborn child' (no. 1).

[27] The 'slippery slope' or 'thin edge of the wedge' argument can be very persuasive, but may be used in almost every circumstance. His questioner might argue that limiting abortions was the top of a slippery slope leading to the loss of equal rights for women (no. 26).

[28] What he really means is that it is the one that will lose him the fewest votes.

[29] C is adopting a position of academic detachment (no. 27) since no matter whether the issue being voted on is the most important one, it still has to be decided one way or the other. However, again, his real reason for detachment is probably the fear of a hostile reaction from one or another group of voters.

Index

1984 132
abstract terms, and concrete
    examples 35–6
academic detachment 116–17, 163–4
advertising 130
Al Qaeda 5
'all' and 'some', omission of 51–61,
    112, 161
'American politician on Russia'
    example 31–3
analogies 118–26
anger 99–100, 163
aphasia 127–8
appeal to mere authority 143, 164
'appeal to nature' analogy 120–1
applause 131–2
argument
    from analogies 118–26, 164
    in circle 82, 162
    from forced analogy 125–6, 164
    from mere analogy 124–5, 126,
        164
    productive 148–50
Aristotle 148
Atkinson, Max 131, 132
attitude of detachment of mind
    109–10

banking analogy 118–19
'beard' example 41, 161
begging the question 82–4, 162
belief systems, dogmatic 152–5
bias 115–16
Bin Laden, Osama 4
biology, and emotional words 12
Bush, George 4, 40

'capital punishment'
    example 56–7
capitalism 154–5
China, use of analogy 123
Christians 4–5
Churchill, Winston 11, 51
circular arguments 82, 162
classification 16, 47–9
codes, and language 15–16
colonialists 6
communism 154–5
comparison of evils, as dishonest
        argument 70–1
concrete examples, of abstract
        terms 35–6
confidence, and suggestion 129,
        132–3, 164
continuous variation 38–43
contrasts 132
conversations, and emotional
        words 10
Copernicus 87
correlations 55–6
'cranks' 95
criticism, literary, and emotional
        words 7
'crusades' example 4–5
'Cuba argument' example 62–3

'damning by association' 79
Darwin, Charles 105, 111
'defensive' weapons 19–20
definitions
    broad 45–6, 47
    difficulties of 37–43
    good and bad 44–50

narrow 46
and valuation 45–7
delivery, manner of 129, 132–3
delusions 77–9, 78–9, 98
democracy
point of view 88
and rational decision 12
'democracy' example 24–5
democratic election analogy 119
dictionary definitions 35–6
discussion, value of 147
dishonest tricks 62–73, 159–64
diversion 66–70, 125, 161–2
dogmatic belief systems 152–5

Einstein, Albert 112
elections 115, 116–17
emotional content, of words 160
emotional language, and poetry 9–10
emotional oratory 10–11, 12, 13
emotional words
and argument of the beard 42
and factual use 2–12, 160
and political discussion 6
practical exercise 13–14
emotions, and prejudice 99–102
equality 156, 157
'The Eve of St Agnes' 9–10
evidence-based research 60–1
evils, comparison of, as dishonest
argument 70–1
'extension', of one's opponent's
statement 63–6, 112, 161

facts, and words 17–28
factual and emotional use of
words 2–12
fallacy of the undistributed
middle 78–9, 112
false credentials, prestige by 134, 164
false quotations 105–6
feminism 156–7
flexibility of mind 95–6

football hooliganism 116
foreign countries 87
'freedom' examples 27, 30–1
Freud, Sigmund 111
fundamentalism 155

Gandhi, Mahatma 4–5
German Nazis 6
Gettysburg address 132
'guerrilla' example 4

habits of thought 85–96
Hall, Radclyffe 7
Heath, Edward 130, 132
hecklers 133
hierarchies 48–9
Hitler, Adolf 103, 134, 151, 152
human rights 156
humanity, common 155
hypnotism 128

inconsequent arguments 69–70, 162
inconsistent opinions 146–8
intellectual experimentation 95–6
intellectual honesty 137
the internet 106
interviews, television 135–6, 137,
165–70
'IQ tests' example 58–9
irrelevant objections 67–9, 125

James, William 17
jargon 139–40, 164
'jihad' 5

Keats, John 9–10
Kennedy, John F. 132

language
and codes 15–16
ways of using 1–2
'language games' 2
'Law of the Excluded Middle' 38–43

League of Nations 151
lesbianism, and emotional words 7–8
Lincoln, Abraham 132
literary criticism, and emotional
    words 7
logical consistency 64, 65–6
logical fallacies 74–84

man and squirrel discussion 17–18
*The Man who Mistook his Wife for a
    Hat* 127
Marx, Karl 154
Marxism 154–5
mathematical example 23–4
mean position between two
    extremes 71–3, 160–1, 162
meanings, of words 29–36
Mein Kampf 103
memory, and prejudice 105–6
metaphors 121, 125
method, of speaking 129, 132–3
mixed metaphors 125
moral judgments, words
    implying 7–9
moral valuation 20–1, 46
Muslims, and 'crusade' 4–5

national names, loose use of 31–4
Nazis 6
1984 132
Nixon, Richard 135
nuclear weapons 19–20

objective truths 87
obscurity, and technical
    language 138–40
oratory, and suggestion 127–37
oratory, emotional 10–11, 12, 13
Orwell, George 132
Our Master's Voices 131

paranoiac delusions 98
paranoid systems 102–4

personal experience, and prestige
    suggestion 143–4
physical theory, and analogies 122
pictures, importance of 155–6
Plato 147
poetry, and emotional language 9–10
point of view 87–93
political discussion, and emotional
    words 6, 12
political propaganda 108–9
predigested thinking 111–17, 163
prejudice 97–110, 163
prejudicial language 156
prestige
    bolstering 138–40, 164
    by false credentials 134, 164
    and public speaking 133–4
prestige suggestion 138–45
productive thinking 148–50
'prohibition' example 51–2
proof by selected instances 55, 56–7,
    60, 155, 161
propaganda 79, 108–9
The Protocols of the Elders of Zion 103
public speaking, and
    suggestion 127–37

quarrels, genesis of 90–3
quotations, false 105–6

'racial differences in IQ' example 58–9
rationalizations 102, 110
Reagan, Ronald 135
'red-haired people' example 52–5
'religion', definition of 45–6
religious thinking, and emotional
    words 6–7
repeated affirmation 129–31, 164
repetition with variation 130–1
The Republic 147
research 60–1
'revolutionary action' example 29–30
Russians 6

American politician's speech
    example 31–3
Sacks, Oliver 127–8
Saddam Hussein 103
sayings 113
scare quotes 23
science
    and analogies 122
    and emotional words 11–12
scientific approach, and public
    confidence 152
shocking ideas 93–4
'sincerity machine' 133
slogans 113–14
'smoking and lung cancer'
    example 55–6
Socrates 147
'some' and 'all', omission of 51–61
Sorensen, Theodore 11
sound bites 132
special pleading 106–8, 163
sport 115–16
squirrel and man discussion 17–18
Stalin, Joseph 152
straight thinking
    future of 151–7
    and inconsistencies 146–8
    and productive argument 148–50
suggestion
    by confident manner 129, 132–3
    and personal experience 143–4
    and predigested phrases 112
    by prestige 138–40, 164
    and public speaking 127–37
    by repeated affirmation 129–31,
        164
syllogism 75–8, 80, 148–9

tautologies 21–3, 160
technical jargon 138–40, 164
technology 152

television
    interviews 135–6, 137, 165–70
    and speeches 132
    and suggestion 134–6
Temperance Act of Scotland 51
tendency 52–5
'terrorism' example 49–50
Thatcher, Margaret 133
thinking, predigested 111–17
thought-habits 85–96
three-part lists 132
tonal Anglia 128
tricks, in argument 62–73, 159–64

undistributed middle 78–9, 112
United Nations 151

valuation
    moral 20–1
    and use of definition 45–7
'vicious' 7–9
Vietnamese incident 6
voting 116–17

wartime 5–6, 114–15
The Well of Loneliness 7
'white paper' example 38–40
Wittgenstein, Ludwig 2
woolliness 35
words
    emotional content 3–12, 42
    and facts 18–28, 160
    implying moral judgments 7–9
    meanings of 29–36
    with no clear meaning 34–5
    right use of 24–6
    with two or more meanings
        29–33